"Homeland *In*Security is a timely and comprehensive examination of the intersection of fear, conspiracy thinking, and violence. Drawing upon The Chapman Survey of American Fears, the authors present a rich and rigorous analysis of the vicious cycle linking fears, real or imagined, to physical attacks on fellow citizens, and government policy responses. This impressive and original volume puts into present-day focus Benjamin Franklin's maxim regarding the tension between liberty and security. As dividing lines continue to harden between adversaries and political violence becomes more frequent, there has never been a greater need for such an instructive book. Anyone with even a passing interest in the roots of political violence in the contemporary United States should give this insightful book a close read."
**Todd L. Belt**, *Professor and Director,*
*Political Management Program, The George Washington University*

"This distressingly timely book uses data from the Chapman University trend study of American Fears to describe what frightens us, especially fears of violence in public spaces like schools, churches, and shopping malls. Then the authors look to recent events and national data to see why those fears are not all that irrational. Finally, however, they describe some positive developments that may give us hope for the future."
**Earl Babbie**, *Campbell Professor Emeritus in Behavioral Sciences, Chapman University*

# Homeland *In*Security

In this book, Ann Gordon and Kai Hamilton Gentry expertly illuminate how the public has a role to play in ensuring its own security.

Recent terror attacks and mass shootings in the United States have added urgency to the need for research on terrorism, the public's understanding of the precursors of terrorism and public preparedness for mass shootings and acts of terror. Unfortunately, most Americans do not understand what constitutes suspicious behavior or how to report it. Even more alarmingly, the public does not know what to do in the event of terrorist attack or mass casualty incident. Drawing on five years of the Chapman Survey of American Fears (CSAF), a nationally representative survey, and real-world events, *Homeland InSecurity* offers actionable solutions on how to educate the public to overcome fear and play an active role securing schools, public venues and the homeland itself. The book addresses proposals by survivors and victims' families to reduce violence through campaigns to deny shooters the notoriety they seek and reduce access to guns. It also explores the rise of activism among survivors of school shootings and their quest to educate the public and end school shootings.

*Homeland* In*Security* will be essential for scholars, students, and policy makers.

**Ann Gordon** is associate professor of political science at Chapman University. She is the director of the Babbie Social Science Research Center and the Ludie and David C. Henley Social Sciences Research Laboratory. She is Co-PI of the ongoing Chapman Survey of American Fears and co-author of *Fear Itself: The Causes and Consequences of Fear in America*.

**Kai Hamilton Gentry** is a recent graduate of Chapman University with a B.A. in political science. He began working on the Chapman Survey of American Fears in 2015, and served as the assistant director of the Henley Social Sciences Research Laboratory. He plans to pursue graduate work in counterterrorism analysis.

# Routledge Research in American Politics and Governance

**Reforming the Presidential Nominating Process**
Front-Loading's Consequences and the National Primary Solution
*Lisa K. Parshall*

**Public Debt and the Common Good**
Philosophical and Institutional Implications of Fiscal Imbalance
*James Odom*

**Removal of the Property Qualification for Voting in the United States**
Strategy and Suffrage
*Justin Moeller and Ronald F. King*

**The Rise of the Republican Right**
From Goldwater to Reagan
*Brian M. Conley*

**Interest Group Design**
The Foundation and Evolution of Common Cause
*Marcie L. Reynolds*

**Pop-Up Civics in 21st Century America**
Understanding the Political Potential of Placemaking
*Ryan Salzman*

**A Tale of Two Parties**
Living Amongst Democrats and Republicans Since 1952
*Kenneth Janda*

**Homeland *In*Security**
Terrorism, Mass Shootings, and the Public
*Ann Gordon and Kai Hamilton Gentry*

# Homeland *In*Security
Terrorism, Mass Shootings, and the Public

**Ann Gordon
and Kai Hamilton Gentry**

NEW YORK AND LONDON

First published 2021
by Routledge
52 Vanderbilt Avenue, New York, NY 10017

and by Routledge
2 Park Square, Milton Park, Abingdon, Oxon, OX14 4RN

*Routledge is an imprint of the Taylor & Francis Group, an informa business*

© 2021 Taylor & Francis

The right of Ann Gordon and Kai Hamilton Gentry to be identified as authors of this work has been asserted by them in accordance with sections 77 and 78 of the Copyright, Designs and Patents Act 1988.

All rights reserved. No part of this book may be reprinted or reproduced or utilised in any form or by any electronic, mechanical, or other means, now known or hereafter invented, including photocopying and recording, or in any information storage or retrieval system, without permission in writing from the publishers.

*Trademark notice*: Product or corporate names may be trademarks or registered trademarks, and are used only for identification and explanation without intent to infringe.

Library of Congress Cataloging-in-Publication Data
A catalog record for this title has been requested

ISBN: 978-0-367-85925-1 (hbk)
ISBN: 978-1-003-01580-2 (ebk)

Typeset in Baskerville
by MPS Limited, Dehradun

To our mothers, Jill and Kathie, for all they have done for us.

# Contents

| | | |
|---|---|---|
| *List of figures and tables* | | *x* |
| *Acknowledgements* | | *xi* |
| 1 | Introduction | 1 |
| 2 | Terrorism | 9 |
| 3 | Mass Shootings | 53 |
| 4 | Conspiracy Theories and Mass Shootings | 78 |
| 5 | Conclusion | 95 |
| | *Index* | 104 |

# List of Figures and Tables

**Figures**

| | | |
|---|---|---|
| 2.1 | Barriers to Reporting | 12 |
| 2.2 | You Notice, but Do You Report? | 14 |
| 2.3 | Terror Attacks and Foiled Plots in the United States, 2014–2018 | 15 |
| 3.1 | Mass Shootings in the United States by Year | 54 |
| 3.2 | Fear of Mass Shootings in the United States by Year | 55 |

**Tables**

| | | |
|---|---|---|
| 3.1 | Buying a Gun Out of Fear by Media Use | 56 |
| 3.2 | A table depicting familiarity with "Stop the Bleed" campaign and active shooter training by demographic characteristics | 63 |
| 4.1 | OLS Regression Predicting Belief in Sandy Hook/Las Vegas/Parkland Conspiracies by Media Use | 82 |
| 4.2 | Belief in the Sandy Hook and South Dakota Crash Conspiracies by Demographics | 83 |

# Acknowledgements

The authors are grateful to so many people who made this book and the Chapman Survey of American Fears possible. The survey is hard work, but Ann's Co-PIs in Chapman's Sociology department, Ed Day and Chris Bader, bring an interdisciplinary perspective and make the project both fun and rewarding. Thanks are also due to Ed for reading earlier versions of this manuscript and providing helpful feedback.

Also, at Chapman, we'd like to thank President Daniele Struppa, Provost Glenn Pfeiffer, Dean Jennifer Keene, and Sarah Gordon for their unwavering support of undergraduate researchers, the fear project, and the Earl Babbie Research Center, at which the CSAF is based. Greg Walswick has gone above and beyond in providing administrative support to the Babbie Center, as has Talisa Flores in support of the Henley Lab.

Our research, and that of so many others, would not be possible without the generosity of Mr. David C. Henley and Mrs. Ludie Henley who founded and support the Henley Lab where the Henley Undergraduate Research Fellows work. These fellows included Shreya Sheth ('21), Syd Kotar ('19), Paige Goedderz ('21), Roxy Amirazizi ('21), Sarah Kashani ('22), and Claire Norman ('19) all of whom provided research assistance. Babbie Center Fellow, Muhammad Karkoutli ('20), assisted with some of the data analysis for this book. Tara Shafie, Irvine High School, assisted in making audio transcriptions and in table making.

We appreciate the help of the Ideation Lab at Chapman University, and its director, Professor Eric Chimenti, who designed figures 2.1 and 2.2 for the chapter on terrorism. The heat map was designed by Claire Norman in the Henley lab.

We also wish to thank Natalja Mortensen, Charlie Baker, and the staff at Routledge for their enthusiasm for this project and for guiding us through the process. Finally, thanks are due to the anonymous reviewers who provided useful comments that improved our work.

# 1 Introduction

Recent terror attacks and mass shootings have shocked and horrified the nation. The nation reeled from two mass shootings in 24 hours, which left dozens of dead, in El Paso, Texas, and Dayton, Ohio. The nation's tragic history of shooting rampages includes Las Vegas, where 58 people died and 851 were injured when a sniper opened fire on an outdoor concert. A little over a year later, a survivor of that shooting was shot and killed in Thousand Oaks, California, at the Borderline Bar and Grill, along with 12 others who died and the 23 who were wounded. Orlando was the location of the deadliest terror attack in the United States since 9/11, where 49 people were killed and another 53 were wounded in a nightclub.[1] Less than a year earlier, in 2015, terrorists attacked a government building in San Bernardino, killing 14 and wounding 22 people. Terror struck the Tree of Life Synagogue in Pittsburgh in 2018, where 11 people were killed and 6 wounded. Not even a year later, at the Chabad of Poway, one woman was killed and three were wounded on the last day of Passover.

The United States has seen the incidence of mass shootings rise. The year 2019 saw more mass shootings than days in the year, with 417 shootings.[2] Even as the nation wrestled with the COVID-19 pandemic in 2020 and widespread stay-at-home orders were issued, mass shootings continued apace.[3] Moreover, the shootings are becoming more deadly.[4] School shootings have risen as well, taking the lives of 356 people in the last 10 years.[5] These attacks have added urgency to the need for research on gun violence, terrorism, the public's understanding of the precursors of terrorism, signs of a school shooter in the making, and public preparedness for the aftermath of mass shootings and acts of terror. Law enforcement agencies work around the clock to anticipate and thwart terrorist attacks, but they cannot do it alone. They rely on the public to provide information. First responders are also aided in saving lives when bystanders are empowered to render aid until professional help arrives.[6]

Thus, following many of these attacks, government officials counseled vigilance and reminded Americans that if they "See Something, Say Something®." Unfortunately, most Americans do not understand what constitutes suspicious behavior or how to report it. Even more alarmingly, the public does not know what to do in the event of terrorist attack or mass casualty incident. Drawing on 5 years of national survey data we have collected and real-world events, this book addresses the need for public education by describing the role the public plays in maintaining its own safety and identifying gaps in the public's knowledge and barriers to collaborating with law enforcement and first responders. We argue that educating the public is key to a safer society, while at the same time preserving civil liberties.

Despite its ubiquity, and high-profile successes, such as locating the Boston bombers, or the Chelsea bomber, the "See Something, Say Something®" campaign has been heavily criticized by the ACLU and others for threatening civil liberties and leading innocent people to be caught up in terror investigations. Due to a lack of information, members of the public often rely on stereotypes and misinformation in determining what constitutes a threat. We demonstrate that educating the public is the best away to avoid reports based on stereotypes and instead receive tips that are based on the actual precursors of terrorism. This helps to reduce reporting that is problematic for civil liberties and less likely to clog up law enforcement process, checking out worthless leads.

Our book addresses the need for public education on how to deal with the immediate aftermath of a shooting or bombing. Bystanders are the first on the scene and knowing what to do to stop the bleeding from wounds normally seen on a battlefield, until help arrives, is a matter of life and death. "Stop the Bleed®" is a federal initiative with the intention of providing bystanders without medical training basic skills and information about steps to take in the case of life-threatening bleeding.[7]

Although we note the role of the mass media in the aforementioned public campaigns, media are also implicated in spurring or inspiring mass shootings and this dynamic will be explored in this book. For example, media heighten fears and fuel firearms sales after mass shootings.[8] Patterns of media usage also play a role in gun purchases that are made out fear. Additionally, shooters seek attention and such media coverage can lead to imitators. As one study notes:

> Importantly, the way that the media report an event can play a role in increasing the probability of imitation. When a mass shooting event occurs, there is generally extensive media coverage. This coverage often repeatedly presents the shooter's image, manifesto, and life story and the details of the event ... and doing so can directly influence imitation.

Social status is conferred when the mass shooter obtains a significant level of notoriety from news reports. Images displaying shooters aiming guns at the camera project an air of danger and toughness.[9]

Because of the importance of media coverage to many shooters and the propensity for such coverage to catalyze attacks, there are proposals by survivors and victims' families to reduce violence through campaigns to deny shooters the notoriety they seek. We also explore the rise of activism among survivors of school shootings and their quest to educate the public, enact legislation, reduce access to guns, and end school shootings. The chief opponent to legislation designed to curb gun violence is the National Rifle Association. As we shall see, this formidable organization is being challenged head on by a new generation of activists.[10]

Complicating the nation's response to terrorism and mass shootings is the widespread belief in conspiracy theories. For example, in 2017, some 26 people were murdered and another 20 were wounded in a church shooting in Sutherland Springs, Texas. Pastor Frank Pomeroy and his wife Sherri lost their teen daughter in the attack.[11] Adding to their grief and trauma was continual harassment by conspiracy theorists. As Pastor Pomeroy explained:

> To be honest, I remember during Sandy Hook hearing about people who were denying the validity and the reality of what had happened up in Sandy Hook ... However, I guess I've never put much credence in those kinds of things and never really listened to it, so I didn't realize just how serious these people can be and how vicious, actually, these people can be when they come down and try to prove their alternate reality. They have been coming to the neighborhood ever since day one, for the most part, and accusing all the neighbors, the parishioners, everyone involved, that we are all traitors to our country because we are trying to carry out a Department of Homeland Security drill to entice the rest of the country to have to live in fear, and that none of our family members or loved ones have existed, that this was all made up and that we are all, each one of us, individually, working together some overall plot against America.[12]

Two conspiracy theorists were arrested after they threatened the Pomeroys. Like many conspiracies related to mass shootings, the theorists wanted to "prove" that the shooting never really happened.[13] Many types of conspiracies circulated about Sutherland Springs, including the belief that the shooting was actually staged by the government in a so-called false flag attack.[14] Most false flag conspiracies include accusations that the government, or some shadowy forces within the government, staged the attack in order to get public support for gun control measures. Far from being unique, these sorts of conspiracy theories have become endemic.

## The Chapman Survey of American Fears

To explore the topics in this book, we rely on The Chapman Survey of American Fears (CSAF). The survey is part of an interdisciplinary research agenda that involves conducting a yearly investigation of fear in the United States through surveys of the American public regarding their fears, the predictors of those fears, their behaviors related to fear, and the consequences of fear on society. The first wave of data was collected in the spring of 2014 and each year thereafter. The CSAF contains detailed demographic information on all respondents, including gender, race, education, employment status, region of the country, marital status, number of children in the household, and age. In the present study, we rely on the first five waves of this unique national survey to explore the public's fear of being the victim of terrorism and mass shootings, and the role education plays in shaping reactions to those fears.[15]

## Fear of Terrorism and Mass Shootings

From mass acts of gun violence at entertainment venues in Las Vegas and Thousand Oaks, to synagogues in Pittsburgh and Poway, and schools like Santa Fe High School in Texas and Marjory Stoneman Douglas High School in Parkland, mass shootings are ever salient in America, with fear of mass shootings reaching an all-time high in 2019, with 47.2% of respondents being afraid or very afraid of personally falling victim to a mass shooting. When we measured this fear in 2015, it was 16.4%. Fear of terrorism peaked in 2014–2015, when terror attacks had been frequent, worldwide, and were covered extensively in the media. Europol reported that there were 211 terror attacks in 2015 on European soil, the highest number since records started in 2006, and these attacks received extensive press coverage in the United States.[16] From 2014–2016, more people in Europe were killed by terror attacks than previous years combined while also commanding the highest average of attacks and plots between the 3 years.[17]

Although fear has risen, preparedness has not. The CSAF data shows that only 21.5% of respondents have had active shooter training at work or in their schools, though some 34.8% are familiar with the advice to "Run. Hide. Fight." when confronted with an active shooter situation. Finally, 28% of the public is familiar or very familiar with the Stop The Bleed®

initiative that is designed to provide first aid to victims of gun violence, until emergency medical services arrive on the scene.

## Overview of the Book

In Chapter 2, we examine the public's fear or terrorism and their familiarity with the See Something, Say Something® Campaign and find that even as awareness of the slogan has increased significantly, public understanding of pre-incident indicators is quite low. Relying on data from the Chapman Survey of American Fears, we look at the likelihood of reporting suspicious activities in the context of a shopping mall. Next, we identify specific barriers to public reporting of suspicious activities that include fear of getting an innocent person in trouble, fear of retaliation, not knowing how to report, and fear they won't be taken seriously. We also identify the best way for these messages to reach the public.

We turn next to America's fear of mass shootings, which has steadily risen since we first began measuring it. In Chapter 3, we explore America's gun problem and proposals by survivors and advocacy groups for gun control measures. The impact of active shooter training on those who have received it is also assessed. We address public knowledge of the "Stop The Bleed®" campaign promoted by doctors and first responders to train bystanders to save lives by treating wounds and blood loss at the scene.

Unfortunately, schools are often the site of mass shootings. Indeed, the United States has had 57 times as many school shootings as Canada, France, Germany, the U.K., Japan, and Italy, *combined*.[18] Thus, there is a school shooting in the United States once a week, on average. In Chapter 3, we will address mass gun violence in schools. Relying on original data from the Chapman Survey of American Fears, we identify attitudes towards school safety and beliefs about the prevalence of violence in schools. Next, we examine the responses to these events and policies advocated by the students, faculty, and community members involved and explore their activism and suggestions regarding gun control. Lastly, we identify the necessity to deny notoriety to perpetrators of mass gun violence because of the potential to incite additional incidents or copycats of previous mass shootings.

In Chapter 4, we explore conspiracy theories linked to mass shootings. With each mass shooting it seems, a conspiracy theory is born. The Chapman Survey of American Fears found that 43% of Americans agree or strongly agree that the government is concealing what it knows about mass shootings such as Sandy Hook, Parkland, and Las Vegas. Following Sandy Hook, conspiracy theorists claimed that "crisis actors" were portraying victims and that none of the carnage was real. Similar claims crop up after each such incident. Moreover, the families of the victims experience unimaginable trauma when they are hounded by conspiracy theorists. The HONR Network was created by Leonard Pozner, whose 6-year-old son Noah was killed in the Sandy Hook shooting. This network was created to end online harassment and to eliminate the many conspiracy theories that flooded the web after Sandy Hook.[19] Bowing to public pressure, YouTube changed its search algorithm after Sandy Hook, to prevent conspiracy theories from finding their way to the top of search results. Nevertheless, conspiracy videos have continued to flourish on YouTube, though the site routinely makes adjustments to combat them.[20] With the proliferation of information on the internet, it can sometimes be difficult to pick out what is and what is not real. Sources are often difficult to verify for laypeople and easily accessible conspiracy theories are available through websites like YouTube, Wordpress, and anonymous message boards like 4chan and Reddit. Conspiracy theories can do real harm. From Sandy Hook to Las Vegas and Parkland, purveyors of conspiracies, such as Infowars host Alex Jones, use their platforms to spread fabrications. Relying on data from our national survey, we explore adherence to conspiracy theories and the relationship between those beliefs and fears of gun control.

We conclude this volume with reflections on Americans' fear and insecurity in their homeland. From schools and entertainment venues, to shopping centers, Americans fear terrorism and mass shootings. These fears are widespread and elevated by America's media consumption habits. However, we find reason to be hopeful in the activism led by survivors and victims' families.

## Notes

1 See Ruth De Foster's excellent study of mass shootings and her analysis of the media construction of terror on why the designation of a shooting as terror is contingent on a variety of factors.
DeFoster 2017.
2 Silverstein 2020.
3 Pryzbyla 2020.
4 Rummler and Lawler 2020.
5 Walker 2019.
6 Department of Homeland Security 2020.
7 Ready 2020.
8 Liu and Wiebe 2019.
9 Meindl and Ivy 2017: 369.
10 Borter 2019.
11 Yan 2017.
12 WBUR 2018.

13 Levin 2018.
14 Hayes 2018.
15 Details on the survey methodology, codebooks, and topline findings are available at: www.chapman.edu/fearsurvey "The Chapman University Survey on American Fears" 2019.
16 BBC News 2016.
17 Nesser, Stenersen, and Oftedal 2016.
18 Grabow and Rose 2018.
19 HONR 2020.
20 Nicas 2017.

## Bibliography

BBC News. "*Record Number of EU Terror Attacks Recorded in 2015.*" July 20, 2016. https://www.bbc.com/news/uk-36845647. Accessed August 5, 2020.

Borter, Gabriella. "*Parkland Massacre Survivors Post Sweeping U.S. Gun-Control Plan Ahead of 2020 Election.*" *Thomson Reuters*, 2019. https://www.reuters.com/article/us-usa-guns/parkland-massacre-survivors-post-sweeping-u-s-gun-control-plan-ahead-of-2020-election-idUSKCN1VB1KE. Accessed August 5, 2020.

*Chapman University*. "The Chapman University Survey on American Fears." 2019. http://www.chapman.edu/fearsurvey. Accessed August 5, 2020.

DeFoster, Ruth. "Mass Shootings in the United States: Mass Media and the Columbine Effect." In *Terrorizing the Masses: Identity, Mass Shootings, and the Media Construction of Terror*, edited by Ruth DeFoster, 17–41. New York: Peter Lang Inc., 2017.

Department of Homeland Security. "*Stop the Bleed.*" 2020. https://www.dhs.gov/stopthebleed. Accessed August 5, 2020.

Grabow, Chip, and Lisa Rose. "*The US Has Had 57 Times as Many School Shootings as the Other Major Industrialized Nations Combined.*" *CNN*, 2018. https://www.cnn.com/2018/05/21/us/school-shooting-us-versus-world-trnd/index.html. Accessed August 5, 2020.

Hayes, Christal. "*Texas Church Shooting Conspiracy Theories Say Gunman Was Muslim Convert, Victims Were Actors.*" *The Guardian*, 2018. https://www.theguardian.com/us-news/2018/mar/06/texas-church-shooting-conspiracy-theorists-arrested. Accessed August 5, 2020.

HONR. "Honor Network Homepage". https://www.honrnetwork.org/. Accessed August 16, 2020.

Levin, Sam. "*Conspiracy Theorists Arrested for Alleged Threats at Site of Texas Church Shooting*". *The Guardian*, 2018. https://www.theguardian.com/us-news/2018/mar/06/texas-church-shooting-conspiracy-theorists-arrested. Accessed August 5, 2020.

Liu, Gina, and Douglas J. Wiebe. "A Time-Series Analysis of Firearm Purchasing After Mass Shooting Events in the United States." *JAMA Network Open 2*, no. 4 (2019): e191736. https://doi.org/10.1001/jamanetworkopen.2019.1736.

Meindl, James N., and Jonathan W. Ivy. "Mass Shootings: The Role of the Media in Promoting Generalized Imitation." *American Journal of Public Health 107*, no. 3 (2017): 368–370. https://doi.org/10.2105/ajph.2016.303611. Accessed August 5, 2020.

Nesser, Petter, Anne Stenersen, and Emilie Oftedal. "Jihadi Terrorism in Europe: The IS-Effect." *Perspectives on Terrorism 10*, no. 6 (2016).

Nicas, Jack. "*YouTube Tweaks Search Results as Las Vegas Conspiracy Theories Rise to Top.*" *Wall Street Journal, Oct. 5, 2017*. https://www.wsj.com/articles/youtube-tweaks-its-search-results-after-rise-of-las-vegas-conspiracy-theories-1507219180. Accessed August 5, 2020.

Przybyla, Heidi. "*Meet the Press Blog: Latest News, Analysis and Data Driving the Political Discussion: Gun violence grows during coronavirus pandemic group's data shows.*" *NBCNews.com*, 2020. https://www.nbcnews.com/politics/meet-the-press/blog/meet-press-blog-latest-news-analysis-data-driving-political-discussion-n988541/ncrd1223551. Accessed August 5, 2020.

Ready. "*You Are the Help Until Help Arrives.*" Ready.gov, 2020. https://www.ready.gov/you-are-help-until-help-arrives. Accessed August 5, 2020.

Rummler, Orion, and Dave Lawler. "*The Deadliest Mass Shootings in Modern U.S. History.*" *Axios*, 2020. https://www.axios.com/deadliest-mass-shootings-modern-us-history-3b2dfb67-7278-4082-a78c-d9fdbef367f1.html. Accessed August 5, 2020.

Silverstein, Jason. "*There Were More Mass Shootings than Days in 2019.*" *CBS News*, 2020. https://www.cbsnews.com/news/mass-shootings-2019-more-than-days-365/. Accessed August 5, 2020.

Walker, Christina. "*10 Years. 180 School Shootings. 356 Victims.*" *CNN*, July 2019. https://www.cnn.com/interactive/2019/07/us/ten-years-of-school-shootings-trnd/. Accessed August 5, 2020.

WBUR. "'*Vicious' Harassment By Conspiracy Theorists After Sutherland Springs Shooting, Pastor Says.*" *Here & Now, March 19*, 2018. https://www.wbur.org/hereandnow/2018/03/19/conspiracy-theorists-sutherland-springs-shooting. Accessed August 5, 2020.

Yan, Holly. "*Sutherland Springs Church Shooting: What We Know.*" *CNN*, November 7, 2017. https://www.cnn.com/2017/11/05/us/texas-church-shooting-what-we-know/index.html. Accessed August 5, 2020.

# 2 Terrorism

An alert beauty store employee named Oscar, contacted authorities after a man made a bulk purchase of acetone and "Ms. Kay's Liquid," a product that contains hydrogen peroxide and is used for bleaching hair.[1] Oscar asked him about his suspicious purchase and the customer explained, "I have a lot of girlfriends."[2] Oscar did not believe that for a second, and was right to be concerned. The man had been trained by al-Qaeda bomb makers in Pakistan to use readily available materials to build bombs, with the goal of attacking the New York subway system on the eighth anniversary of the 9/11 attacks.[3] He had taken the peroxide and acetone, along with muriatic acid, which is used for swimming pools and had easily been purchased at Lowe's, to his $40/night room at Homestead Suites in Aurora, Colorado. There, he mixed up a powerful explosive known as TATP. He made enough for three explosive devices that would be hidden in backpacks.[4] This case is an example of the role the public can play in assisting law enforcement.[5]

## Foiled Attacks and the Role of Public Information

As the New York subway case described illustrates, public tips are an important element in uncovering and stopping terror attacks. About 19% of foiled plots involve information from the public and about 4% of attacks carried out were found to have been reported.[6] For example, in a case similar to the subway plot, a Saudi national, who was a student at Texas Tech University, was arrested after a chemical company tipped off the FBI, due to a suspicious order.[7] He had already obtained two out of three chemicals needed to make a bomb and had a list of targets in the United States.

One study of over 300 terror cases found that 32% were uncovered because the would-be attackers actually spoke or wrote about their plans.[8] For example, a citizen reported alarming Facebook posts to the FBI. The posts included, "Getting ready to be killed in jihad is a HUGE adrenaline rush!! I am so nervous. NOT because I'm scared to die but I am eager to meet my lord." The posts had been made by a Topeka, Kansas, man who admitted to the FBI that he had joined the military, planning a copycat of the Ft. Hood terror attacks committed by an Army Major.[9]

Facebook posts also played a role in apprehending a Florida man who had planned to use a backpack bomb full of nails on a Key West beach and was trying to recruit for ISIS through Facebook. The Palm Beach County sherriff was contacted by a resident who reported receiving a friend request from a man who was attempting to recruit for ISIS.[10]

## If You See Something, Say Something Campaign®

To increase the vigilance on the part of the public, the Department of Homeland Security has a campaign to remind people, "If you see something, say something." We now turn to an exploration of that program and the effectiveness of the messaging strategy. The "See Something, Say Something®" campaign is a nationwide effort led by the Department of Homeland Security to raise public awareness of terrorism and terrorism-related crime. It began in 2010 and was re-launched and expanded in 2015, with public service announcements featuring NASCAR drivers.

The campaign has worked with many such partners to spread the message, including hotel chains and the NFL. Indeed, the campaign launched at Super Bowl XLV, utilizing a variety of techniques from billboards to mobile apps and print sources. In addition to nationwide messaging, regional efforts have also been led by local law enforcement agencies. For example, in Orange County, CA, the Santa Ana and Anaheim police departments created a campaign using a 10-foot-tall red backpack that was placed at the Orange County Fair and other highly visible locations. It was a very tangible embodiment of the idea that the public should report something that does not seem right, such as an unattended backpack. Along with the backpack came public service announcements, a website, and other public outreach materials. On national "If You See Something, Say Something®" Awareness Day, September 25th, 2017, DHS added an infographic with examples of suspicious activity. It includes a variety of indicators, such as eliciting information, materials acquisition of storage, and surveillance. There are 15 indicators on the infographic.[11] As we shall see, this is an important next step in developing awareness, as most people are unsure what to report.

## Public Familiarity with the If You See Something, Say Something Campaign®

Public awareness of the slogan, "If You See Something, Say Something®" has increased due to national and local efforts. In 2013, a Gallup poll reported that only 13% of Americans identified the slogan as relating to terrorism or crime (12%). The poll found that the majority of Americans (55%) had not heard of it at all.[12] However, just 3 years later, awareness had skyrocketed. The Chapman Survey of American Fears found that 92% of Americans believe it refers to terrorism and crime (91%). Just 15% told us they were unsure of what the slogan means.[13]

## How Is the Message Reaching the Public?

The public has become familiar with the slogan through a variety of outreach efforts. The single biggest source of information was television for 58% of Americans. About a third heard the slogan via social media or the web (32%); a third heard it in person in talks given by law enforcement (31%); and some 29% saw or heard the slogan and a concert, sporting event, or fair. It is clear that no single channel of communication should be used. Rather, it is a combination of outreach efforts that has achieved high visibility for the slogan and idea of being alert and reporting. Multiple communication methods will be needed to continue to educate the public on precursors, as the slogan alone raises awareness, but does not assist members of the public in pinpointing what should be a cause for concern.

## Americans Fear Retaliation If They Report Suspicious Activities

There are a number of factors that may impede reporting of suspicious activities, as well as some that would increase the likelihood of reporting. The concerns we examined were fear of retaliation, getting an innocent person in trouble, not knowing how to report, and not being taken seriously. We also asked whether respondents believed there was no need to report suspicious activity because someone else would do it and if they felt, "It is not my responsibility to watch for suspicious activity."

The top fear was retaliation for 55.1% of Americans (see Figure 2.1). This is an area that should be clearly addressed in any public outreach efforts and anonymous reporting should be highlighted and be readily available in all jurisdictions to remove this as a barrier to reporting suspicious activity. The second biggest concern (45.9%) centered on the fear of getting an innocent person in trouble. There may be a good basis for this

| I would not report because... | % AGREE | % DISAGREE |
|---|---|---|
| Get an innocent person in trouble | 45.9 | 54.1 |
| Fears retaliation | 55.1 | 44.9 |
| Does not know how to report | 28.5 | 71.6 |
| Won't be taken seriously | 25.8 | 71.6 |
| Someone else will do it | 13.4 | 86.6 |
| Not my responsibility | 19.3 | 80.7 |

⬢ = Less likely to report    ⬢ = more likely to report

*Figure 2.1* Barriers to Reporting.
Source: CSAF, Wave 3, $N = 1511$.

worry, as the See Something, Say Something® program has been challenged in the courts due to innocent people being caught up in investigations. We will return to this topic later in the chapter.

Encouragingly, the vast majority of respondents disagreed that someone else would report (86.6%) and they overwhelmingly (80.7%) rejected the statement that is it not "my responsibility." Thus, Americans do believe that it is their responsibility to report suspicious activity that they see and they do not believe in letting someone else do it. Notably, some 28.5% of Americans told us they would not know how to report their observations. This is an area where additional education efforts could focus. Another 25.8% worried they would not be taken seriously, so this concern should also be addressed in public information campaigns.

## Public Awareness of Potential Indicators of Terrorist Activities Related to Shopping Malls and Centers

Having investigated the public's familiarity with the See Something, Say Something® campaign, we now look more deeply into public perceptions of what constitutes suspicious activity and the likelihood of reporting such behaviors. The scenarios tested were drawn from the Department of Justice fact sheet on what should be considered suspicious in the context of a mall as well as other If You See Something, Say Something® materials. These behaviors include: unusual inquiries about security procedures, individual(s) with unseasonal bulky attire, unattended packages, briefcases, satchels or bags, extremist graffiti spray-painted at the center, efforts to surveil or "case" the shopping center, unattended vehicles parked in front of store entrances, people and actions that are out of place, and awareness of demonstrations conducted at the mall. Additional suspicious behaviors were included were unusual smells or smoke that is worrisome and tampering with a smoke detector and using chairs to block exits were also included.

It is also critical to educate the public on what should not be reported. "The campaign does not promote spying on others or making judgments based on a person's race, ethnicity, national origin, or religious affiliation. Residents are encouraged to report situations and behavior as possible terrorist or violent acts rather than beliefs, thoughts, ideas, expressions, associations, or speech unrelated to criminal activity." Therefore, we included examples of free speech such has handing out the Koran, and people hanging out by a fountain. Additionally, we included a scenario of an individual with Nazi tattoos hanging out in front of the mall, a sight that is troubling, but should not be reported. Finally, we asked respondents about familiar crimes such as witnessing a shoplifter and an individual breaking into a car in the mall's parking lot.

Respondents were most likely to say they would report crimes such as shoplifting (73.7%) or breaking into a car (84.4%), followed by reporting a chemical smell and smoke at (79%). Far less likely to be regarded as suspicious are people and actions that are out of place. In the scenario presented, "Two people are standing around near a concert taking place at the mall, but appear to have no interest in the concert"; some 8.5% of respondents would deem that suspicious enough to report. The number jumps to 51.2% when the people are described as "… two young people who appear very nervous, and one stutters when you say hello. They are constantly looking over their shoulders and are sweating profusely." Another out-of-place example was, "You notice someone wearing a heavy overcoat, even though it is a very hot day." Around 37.5% of respondents would report this (Figure 2.2).

Efforts to surveil the mall are not broadly recognized as behavior that should be reported, especially when compared to the numbers for reporting shoplifting and breaking into a car. For example, a stranger asking how often "mall security walks through this part of the mall" would be reported by 39.8% of respondents. The number increases to 47.4% for "a man using his smart phone to take pictures of mall security cameras." Unusual inquiries about security procedures would be reported by 39.8% of respondents.

A majority would report an unattended backpack (57.8%), chairs blocking exits (54.9%), and a smoke detector being disabled (54.5%), but only 33.2% would see a truck "left in a No Parking zone directly in front of the mall" as suspicious activity that they would be likely to report. "Freshly spray-painted, Anti-American slogans on a wall" would be reported by 43.7% of respondents.

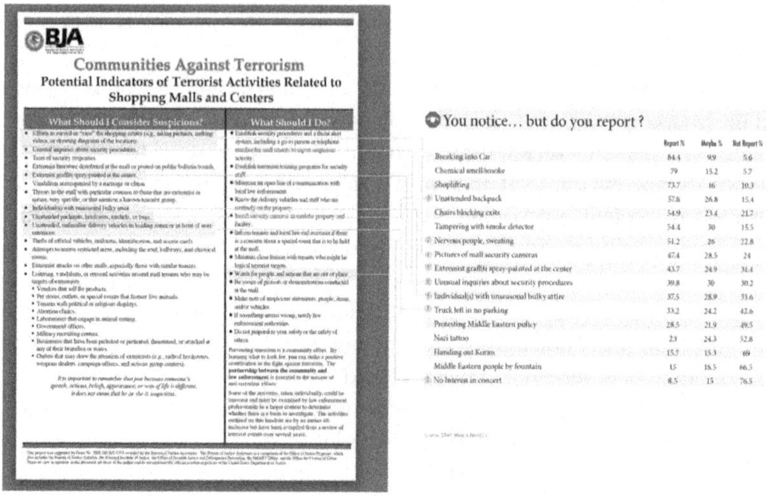

*Figure 2.2* You Notice, but Do You Report?

Encouragingly, the majority of respondents did not see freedom of speech and assembly examples as suspicious. Handing out the Koran would not be reported by 69% of respondents, nor would Middle Eastern people assembled by a fountain (66.5%) or individuals with Nazi tattoos (52.8%).

## Public Perceptions of Terrorists

The public fears both Islamic Extremism/Jihadists and White Supremacists, with 49% of the public (overall) perceiving each to be a threat to national security.[14] That the public sees both of these groups as equally threatening is supported by data on terrorist incidents in the United States. Some 19% of foiled plots from 1995 to 2012 were motivated by Al Quaeda supporters and affiliated movements, 20% were linked to white supremacists, and 17% were militia/anti-government militia movements.[15] In Figure 2.3, we have mapped out the location of terror attacks and foiled terror plots in the United States from 2014–2018. On our map, 30% of the plots or foiled plots were Muslim Extremists/Jihadis and 37.4% were White Supremacist and other far-right extremists.[16] The map also includes an "other" category (15.4%), where the attacker was not caught and the motive is unknown (majority of these incidents were church fires, followed by mass shootings/shooting sprees that were attacks on journalists, newspapers, and companies like YouTube). Additionally, these

*Figure 2.3* Terror Attacks and Foiled Plots in the United States, 2014–2018. For source, see "List of Completed and Foiled Terror Plots and Citations Used to Create Terror Map" at the end of the chapter.

incidents also included attacks on municipal buildings and airports, anti-pornography arson, and mail attacks. An additional 8.9% of the map includes anti-police violence. Finally, 6.5% is accounted for by anarchists, environmentalists, and other far-left extremists.

The Trump Administration was out of touch with both public sentiments and compelling data in their reluctance to call violence perpetrated by white supremacists terrorism for years after taking office. Trump himself had set the tone for his political appointees to follow. It was not until a spate of horrific shootings, motivated by white supremacist ideology, that DHS finally acknowledged the domestic terror threat in 2019.[2]

## Trump's Response to Charlottesville

White supremacists descended upon Charlottesville, Virginia, on August 11th and 12th, 2017. They marched with swastika flags and symbols of the confederacy. The "Unite the Right" rally was meant to bring together all manner of far-right extremists, the alt-right, and racists. The pretense was a protest of the removal of a Robert E. Lee statue from a public park. The statue had been slated for removal as part of a nationwide response to the horrific slaying of nine members of the Emanual A.M.E. Church in Charleston, South Carolina, by a white supremacist who was hoping to start a race war.[17] All over the country, symbols of hatred were coming down. For example, the University of Mississippi took down its state flag, which has the same confederate battle emblem that the Charleston shooter posed with in pictures.[18]

The "Unite the Right" rally was violent, as many of the white supremacists had long been preparing and came to the event armed:

> But the white supremacists who flooded into the city's Emancipation Park—a statue of Confederate General Robert E. Lee sits in the center of the park—had spent months openly planning for war. The Daily Stormer, a popular neo-Nazi website, encouraged rally attendees to bring shields, pepper spray, and fascist flags and flagpoles. A prominent racist podcast told its listeners to come carrying guns. "Bring whatever you need, that you feel you need for your self defense. Do what you need to do for security of your own person," said Mike "Enoch" Peinovich on The Right Stuff podcast.[19]

It was widely reported that the police observed but did little to prevent the violence. Before it was all over, the governor had declared a state of emergency and 32-year-old Heather Heyer was killed and dozens injured, when one of the white supremacists drove his car into a crowd of peaceful counter-protesters.[20]

Rather than condemning the white supremacists, Nazis, and their hateful ideology, President Trump found blame on "many sides." The backlash was swift and multiple attempts by the White House to clean up or reframe Trump's comments fell flat, as Trump himself continued to reiterate his belief that "I think there is blame on both sides."[21] Some two years later, Trump was still defending his position. "If you look at what I said, you will see that that question was answered perfectly ... I was talking about people who went because they felt very strongly about the monument to Robert E. Lee, a great general."[22]

It is not just Trump's rhetoric that is troubling, but also the actions taken by his administration. Indeed, a Trump appointee who runs the DHS Office of Intelligence and Analysis shut down the division tasked with informing local law enforcement about threats from violent extremism and domestic terrorists. Because of this, local law enforcement saw a noticeable drop in information sharing and outreach efforts, such as seminars and workshops.[23]

Downplaying violence by domestic extremist groups is the wrong approach, as researchers at the Brookings Institute have pointed out:

> Words matter, but deeds matter more. It is all well and good to label left- and right-wing violence at home as terrorism, but what if the U.S. government went beyond rhetoric and truly treated these groups as it treats Americans suspected of being involved with jihadist organizations like ISIS? The differences would be profound. Not only would the resources that law enforcement devotes to nonjihadist groups soar, but so too would the means of countering those groups. The legal toolkit

would grow dramatically. Perhaps as important would be the indirect effects: banks, Internet companies, and other organizations vital to any group's success would shy away from anything smacking of domestic terrorism. Nonviolent groups that share some of the radicals' agenda would also face pressure, and many would feel compelled to change, often in ways that go against U.S. ideals of free speech and free assembly.[24]

The Trump Administration's approach to terrorism and President Trump's refusal to acknowledge and denounce violence by white supremacists and Nazis has led to a predictable difference in how partisans view terrorism. More than 80% of Republican Party identifiers say Islamic Extremists/Jihadists are a threat to national security; whereas Independents and moderate Democrats average just 50%, and 42% of strong Democrats see these groups as a threat to national security. Fear of white supremacists is the mirror opposite: some 34% of moderate Republicans and 36% of strong Republicans view them as a threat. The number who fear white supremacists rises to 44% among Independents, 73% among moderate Democrats, and 74% among strong Democrats.[25] Being alert and objective about potential indicators of terrorist activity, and then reporting that suspicious activity, is difficult if partisanship in the lens through which the public views threats. As we shall see, suspicious activity reporting has often relied on impressions formed through prejudice, leading to appalling civil liberties violations.

## Suspicious Activity Reports and Fusion Centers

We now turn to an exploration of where information goes when someone reports suspicious activity. Following 9/11, a bipartisan commission was formed, *The National Commission on Terrorist Attacks Upon the United States*, often called *The 9/11 Commission*.

It investigated the profound failure to detect and disrupt the planned attacks. They pointed to a range of factors from a failure of "imagination" to specific issues within the FBI, the CIA, immigration authorities, the Defense department, and the slow response from Congress and the executive branch. One area of special concern was the inability to "connect the dots" prior to the attacks. Doing so would have painted a very clear picture of the threat. In their report, the 9/11 Commission stated, "The U.S. government has access to a vast amount of information. But it has a weak system for processing and using what it has. The system of "need to know" should be replaced by a system of "need to share."[26] Part of the response to this observation was the creation of fusion centers. These would be regional centers around the country tasked with coordinating intelligence gathering and assessment from state and local law enforcement and federal agencies. There are now 79 such centers around the country, funded by the Department of Homeland Security (itself a response to recommendations of the 9/11 Commission).

Along with the creation of fusion centers came the Nationwide Suspicious Activity Reporting Initiative. It provides a framework for how information is collected and shared through suspicious activity reports, or SARs. In a briefing for members of Congress, prepared by the Congressional Research Service, the way a SAR should be handled is described:

> When a police officer detects suspicious activity that might be terrorist related, he or she documents that activity in a SAR. That report is reviewed within the officer's chain of command. Once vetted, it is submitted to a state/local fusion center, where it is reviewed by an intelligence analyst to determine whether it meets the established SAR criteria. If so, the report is entered into the information-sharing environment, where it becomes accessible to authorized agencies at all levels of government and available for analysis and fusion with other intelligence information.[27]

This process for reporting activity that could be linked to terrorism had some successes in uncovering terror plots, as well as criminal activity such as sex trafficking.[28] For example, the North Carolina Information Sharing & Analysis [Fusion] Center caught a 24-year-old North Carolina man, who had been trained by terrorists in Pakistan and Afghanistan.[29] He:

> ... conspired to provide material support and resources to terrorists, including currency, training, transportation and personnel. The object of the conspiracy, according to the indictment, was to advance violent *jihad*, including supporting and participating in terrorist activities abroad and committing acts of murder, kidnapping or maiming persons abroad ... as part of the conspiracy, Boyd assisted other defendants as they prepared themselves to engage in violent *jihad* and were willing to die as martyrs. They also allegedly offered training in weapons and financing, and helped arrange overseas travel and contacts so others could wage violent *jihad* overseas. In addition, as part of the conspiracy, the defendants raised money to support training efforts, disguised the destination of such monies from the donors and obtained assault weapons to develop skills with the weapons. Some defendants also allegedly radicalized others to believe that violent jihad was a personal religious obligation.[30]

Despite examples such as the one above, there has been significant criticism of fusion centers for everything from wasteful spending to spying on war protestors. The problem was summed up in a bipartisan report produced by the U.S. Senate Permanent Subcommittee on Investigations which found:

> ... DHS intelligence officers assigned to state and local fusion centers produced intelligence of "uneven quality – oftentimes shoddy, rarely timely, sometimes endangering citizens' civil liberties and Privacy Act protections, occasionally taken from already-published public sources, and more often than not unrelated to terrorism."[31]

The civil liberties violations noted above have been the subject of lawsuits. For example, the ACLU filed a lawsuit, *Gil v. DOJ*, on behalf of five people who were the subjects of suspicious activity reports. The ACLU claims that the people they represent, "were all engaging in innocuous, lawful, and in some cases First Amendment–protected activity, such as photographing sites of aesthetic interest, playing video games, and waiting at a train station."[32] Although the ACLU ultimately lost the case, we can gain some valuable insight from the details. For example, the train station incident referenced above involved a U.S. citizen, Tariq Razak, of Pakistani descent, who had gone to the Santa Ana train station to apply for a job. A security guard noted that he was of Middle Eastern descent and that he was accompanied by a woman in a "white burka headdress" (actually it was a hijab and the woman was his mother). The guard thought he was behaving suspiciously and that he was "surveying" the entrance and exit to the train station. In reality, he was looking around for the location of his appointment, having never been to the train station.[33] What becomes clear in the court filings is that, more than anything else, Mr. Razak was targeted because of his appearance and his mother's clothing. In the absence of better education, reports like these, which rely on prejudice and stereotypes, will continue to threaten civil liberties. Given that fusion centers and SARs are here to stay, we argue that an important improvement in the quality of reports can only be made through significant efforts at better educating the public—and security personnel for that matter—so that they know what should actually be reported (the bulk purchase of acetone, peroxide, and pool acid comes to mind).[34]

## Conclusion

The balance between democratic values and safety is clearly a fraught issue for the public. The CSAF found one-third of Americans agree or strongly agree with the statement, "In order to curb terrorism in this country, it will be necessary to give up some civil liberties." Even more, 35% disagree or strongly disagree with the statement, "We should preserve our freedoms even if it increases the risk of terrorism." As has been seen before, elevated fears over national security can lead to lower support for national values, a trend that should trouble all Americans. As we demonstrated elsewhere, fear is particularly virulent when it arises out of a sense of powerlessness.[35] To reduce fear of terrorism and the concomitant willingness to give up civil liberties and the most cherished value in America, freedom, the public must regain some sense of control. An educated public that feels equipped to recognize legitimate precursors of terrorist activity, will be more likely to forward useful tips to law enforcement and less likely to stew in their insecurity.

## Notes

1  Ross, Esposito, Sandell, and Schwartz 2009; Cardona and Finley 206.
2  Glaeser 2019.
3  Meyer 2019.
4  Apuzzo and Goldman 2013.
5  In addition to making suspicious purchases, the would-be bomber had been sending emails to known terrorists in Pakistan, and this had landed him on law enforcement's radar.
6  Strom, Hollywood, and Pope 2017.
7  Mckinley and Wheaton 2019.
8  Gomez 2019.
9  Dulle 2015.
10 Department of Justice 2017.
11 Department of Homeland Security 2019.
12 Ander and Swift 2013.
13 CSAF, Wave 3, conducted in 2016; Ander and Swift 2013.
14 CSAF, Wave 5, 2018.
15 Strom, Hollywood, and Pope 2017.
16 Special thanks to Claire Norman, Henley Lab Research Fellow, Chapman class of 2019, for creating the map and data-set. For a list of cases used and sources, see Appendix.
17 McGill 2017.
18 Starr 2019.
19 Thompson 2019.
20 Burke and Sotomayor 2018.
21 Merica 2019.
22 Ibid.
23 Woodruff 2019.
24 Byman 2019.
25 CSAF, Wave 4, 2017.
26 National Commission on Terrorist Attacks Upon the United States 2004.
27 Bjelopera 2011: 7–8.
28 Department of Homeland Security 2015.

29  Peteritas 2013.
30  Department of Justice 2016.
31  Permanent Subcommittee on Investigations 2012.
32  ACLU 2014.
33  ACLU of Northern California 2016.
34  It is not a goal of this chapter to provide a comprehensive critique of fusion centers and SARs. Rather, we want to underscore that the quality of information received, impacts the ability of centers to detect terrorist activities, and reduces the need to run down tips that are worthless at best and civil rights violations at worst.
35  Bader et al. 2020.

## BibliographySwift

ACLU. "*Gill v. DOJ – Challenge to Government's Suspicious Activity Reporting Program.*" July 11, 2014. https://www.aclu.org/cases/gill-v-doj-challenge-governments-suspicious-activity-reporting-program. Accessed May14, 2019.

ACLU of Northern California. "*Gill v. DOJ (Challenge to Federal Suspicious Activity Reporting)*." December 8, 2016. https://www.aclunc.org/our-work/legal-docket/gill-v-doj-challenge-federal-suspicious-activity-reporting. Accessed May14, 2019.

Ander, Steve, and Art Swift. "'*See Something, Say Something' Unfamiliar to Most Americans.*" *Gallup*, December 23, 2013. https://news.gallup.com/poll/166622/something-say-something-unfamiliar-americans.aspx. Accessed August15, 2020.

Apuzzo, Matt, and Adam Goldman. *Enemies Within: Inside the NYPD's Secret Spying Unit and Bin Laden's Final Plot Against America*. United Kingdom: Atria Books, 2013.

Bader, C., Day, L.E., Gordon, A. *Chapman Survey of American Fears*, Earl Babbie Research Center, Chapman University, Wave 2, 2015.

Bader, Chris, Joseph O. Baker, L. Edward Day, and Ann Gordon. *Fear Itself: Causes and Consequences of Fear in American*. New York: NYU Press, 2020.

Bjelopera, Jerome P. "*Terrorism Information Sharing and the Nationwide Suspicious Activity Report Initiative: Background and Issues for Congress.*" *Congressional Research Service*, December 28, 2011. https://fas.org/sgp/crs/intel/R40901.pdf. Accessed May13, 2019.

Burke, Minyvonne, and Marianna Sotomayor. "*Driver Who Plowed into Crowd at Charlottesville Rally Guilty of First-degree Murder.*" *NBCNews.com*, December 7, 2018. https://www.nbcnews.com/news/crime-courts/james-alex-fields-found-guilty-killing-heather-heyer-during-violent-n945186. Accessed June3, 2019.

Byman, Daniel L. "*Should We Treat Domestic Terrorists the Way We Treat ISIS?: What Works- and What Doesn't.*" *Brookings*, October 6, 2017. https://www.brookings.edu/articles/should-we-treat-domestic-terrorists-the-way-we-treat-sis-what-works-and-what-doesnt/. Accessed May9, 2019.

Cardona, Felisa, and Bruce Finley. "*Feds: Aurora Terror Suspect Shopped for Bomb Materials Beauty-supply Stores.*" *Denver Post*, May 7, 2016. https://www.denverpost.com/2009/09/24/feds-aurora-terror-suspect-shopped-for-bomb-materials-beauty-supply-stores/. Accessed May9, 2019.

Department of Homeland Security. *"Fusion Center Success Stories."* July 23, 2015. https://www.dhs.gov/fusion-center-success-stories. Accessed May14, 2019.

Department of Homeland Security. *"If You See Something, Say Something Indicators Infographic (full)."* May 8, 2019. https://www.dhs.gov/see-something-say-something/recognize-the-signs. Accessed May9, 2019.

Department of Justice. *"Florida Man Convicted at Trial of Attempting to Use a Weapon of Mass Destruction and Providing Material Support to ISIL."* January 31, 2017. https://www.justice.gov/opa/pr/florida-man-convicted-trial-attempting-use-weapon-mass-destruction-and-attempting-provide. Accessed May9, 2019.

Department of Justice. *"North Carolina Man Pleads Guilty to Terrorism Charge."* January 8, 2016. https://www.justice.gov/opa/pr/north-carolina-man-pleads-guilty-terrorism-charge-0. Accessed May14, 2019.

Dulle, Brian. *"Topeka Man Arrested for Planning Attack on Ft. Riley on Behalf of ISIS."* KSNT, April 10, 2015. https://www.ksnt.com/news/kansas/topeka-man-arrested-for-planning-attack-on-ft-riley-on-behalf-of-isis_2018030906310846/1023835326. Accessed May9, 2019.

Glaeser, Katie. *"Terror Suspect Stocked up Beauty Supplies."* CNN, September 25, 2009. http://www.cnn.com/2009/CRIME/09/24/terror.indictment/index.html. Accessed May9, 2019.

Gomez, Alan. *"N.Y.-Area Bombings Raise Immigrant Screening Concerns."* USA Today, September 19, 2016. https://www.usatoday.com/story/news/nation/2016/09/19/terror-bombings-raise-immigrant-security-screening-concerns/90708704/. Accessed May9, 2019.

Jackson, David. *"Trump Defends Response to Charlottesville Violence, Says He Put It 'Perfectly' with 'Both Sides' Remark."* USA Today, April 26, 2019. https://www.usatoday.com/story/news/politics/2019/04/26/trump-says-both-sides-charlottesville-remark-said-perfectly/3586024002/. Accessed June3, 2019.

McGill, Kevin, and Associated Press. *"Analysis: Did the Emanuel AME Church Massacre Push New Orleans to Remove Confederate Monuments?"* Post and Courier, May 14, 2017. https://www.postandcourier.com/news/analysis-did-the-emanuel-ame-church-massacre-push-new-orleans/article_25c9b8b8-38e7-11e7-b401-8b4b0e2321e8.html. Accessed June3, 2019.

Mckinley, James C., and Sarah Wheaton. *"Saudi Student to Be Arraigned in Bomb Plot."* New York Times, February 25, 2011. https://www.nytimes.com/2011/02/26/us/26texas.html. Accessed May9, 2019.

Merica, Dan. *"Trump: 'Both Sides' to Blame for Charlottesville."* CNN, August 16, 2017. https://www.cnn.com/2017/08/15/politics/trump-charlottesville-delay/index.html. Accessed June3, 2019.

Meyer, Jeremy P. *"Meyer: Najibullah Zazi, the Terrorist Who Lived Next Door."* Denver Post, November 27, 2015. https://www.denverpost.com/2015/11/27/meyer-najibullah-zazi-the-terrorist-who-lived-next-door/. Accessed May9, 2019.

National Commission on Terrorist Attacks Upon the United States. *"The 9/11 Commission Report."* 2004. http://govinfo.library.unt.edu/911/report/911Report_Exec.htm. Accessed May14, 2019.

Permanent Subcommittee on Investigations. *"Home Security & Governmental Affairs."*

October 3, 2012. https://www.hsgac.senate.gov/imo/media/doc/10-3-2012%20PSI%20STAFF%20REPORT%20re%20FUSION%20CENTERS.2.pdf Accessed. May14, 2019.

Peteritas, Brian. 2013. *"Fusion Centers Struggle to Find Their Place in the Post-9/11 World."* Governing, June 2013. https://www.governing.com/topics/public-justice-safety/gov-fusion-centers-post-911-world.html. Accessed May14, 2019.

Ross, Brian, Richard Esposito, Clayton Sandell, and Rhonda Schwartz. *"The Beauty Parlor Bomb Plan; Massive Terror Plot Alleged."* ABC News, September 24, 2009. https://abcnews.go.com/Blotter/zazi-arrest-nyc-terror-plot-suspect-bought-chemicals/story?id=8662211. Accessed May9, 2019.

Starr, Alexandra. *"University Of Mississippi Orders State Flag Removed."* NPR, October 26, 2015. https://www.npr.org/sections/thetwo-way/2015/10/26/451955764/university-of-mississippi-orders-state-flag-removed. Accessed June3, 2019.

Strom, Kevin J., John S. Hollywood, and Mark Pope. "Terrorist Plots in the United States: What We have Really Faced, and How We Might Best Defend against It." In *The Handbook of the Criminology of Terrorism, edited by Gary LaFree and Joshua D. Freilich, 468-481*. Malden, MA: Wiley Blackwell, 2017.

Swift, Steve Ander and Art. *'See Something, Say Something' Unfamiliar to Most Americans. Gallup.com, Gallup*, September 10, 2020. http://www.gallup.com/poll/166622/something-say-something-unfamiliar-americans.aspx.

Thompson, A.C. *"Police Stood By as Mayhem Mounted in Charlottesville."* ProPublica, August 12, 2017. https://www.propublica.org/article/police-stood-by-as-mayhem-mounted-in-charlottesville. Accessed June3, 2019.

Woodruff, Betsy. *"Homeland Security Disbands Domestic Terror Intelligence Unit."* Daily Beast, April 2, 2019. https://www.thedailybeast.com/homeland-security-disbands-domestic-terror-intelligence-unit. Accessed May9, 2019.

## Appendix List of Completed and Foiled Terror Plots and Citations Used to Create Terror Map

### 2014

**Arvada, Colorado***(18, Female, USA)* Provided material and personnel support to ISIS, Al-Qaeda, and FTOs in Iraq

**Hattiesburg, Mississippi***\*No one was arrested for the incident\* Anti-Muslim shooting*

**Katy, Texas***(38, Male, White, USA)Anti-government inspired explosive terror plot*

**Bunkerville, Nevada***(68, Male, White, USA) Anti-government armed standoff*

**Raleigh, North Carolina** *(19–20, Male, USA) (21–22, Male, USA) Provided Personnel Support to ISIS*

**Orland Park, Illinois***\*No one was arrested for the incident\* Anti-Muslim shooting*

**Rochester, New York***(30, Male, USA) Provided Personnel Support, planned a terror plot for ISIS*

**Overland Park, Kansas***(72, Male, White, USA) Anti-Semitic shooting*

*(Continued)*

**Vero Beach, Florida**(18, Male, Palestinian, USA) Suicide bombing for al-Nusra Front

**Seattle, Washington**(34, Male, USA) Muslim extremist shooting

**Acampo, California**(20, Male, White, USA) Provided personnel support to ISIL

**Cumming, Georgia**(48, Male, White, USA) Anti-government shooting by the Sovereign Citizens

**Las Vegas, Nevada**(31, Male, USA) (22, Female, USA) Anti-government shooting

**Nevada City, California**(60, Male, White, USA) Right-wing extremist shooting

**Tremonton, Utah**(47, Male, White, USA) Anti-government, neo-Nazi explosive terror plot

**Dallas, Texas**(60, Male, White, USA) Anti-government shooting

**Kansas City, Missouri**(27, Male, White, USA) Anarchist explosion

**Chicago, Illinois**(19, Male, USA) Provided personnel support to ISIL

**New York City, New York**\*No one was arrested for the incident\* Anti-Putin armed assault

**Madison, Wisconsin**(33, Male, White, USA) Provided personnel support to ISIL

**Coachella, California**Anti-Muslim shooting

**Glen Allen, Virginia**(28, Female, White, USA) Provided material support to ISIS

**Los Angeles, California**(55, Male, African American, USA) Anti-police arson

**Minneapolis, Minnesota**(17, Male, USA) (19, Male, Somalian, Somalia and USA) Provided material support to ISIL

**Weirton, West Virginia**(22, Male, White, USA) Explosive terror plot

**Isla Vista, California**(22, Male, Chinese-American, USA) Misogynistic, racist mass shooting

**Nogales, Arizona**\*No one was arrested for the incident\* Explosion

**San Diego, California**(28, Male, African American, USA) Provided personnel support to ISIS

**Orange, California**(20, Male, USA) Provided personnel support to ISIL

**North Carolina**(44, Male, White, USA) Provided personnel support to ISIL

**West Orange, New Jersey** (29, Male, USA) Muslim extremist shooting

**Blooming Grove, Pennsylvania**(30, Male, White, USA) Anti-government shooting

**Queens, New York**(32, Male, African American, USA) Armed assault inspired by Muslim extremism

**Albuquerque, New Mexico**\*No one was arrested for the incident\* Anti-Muslim explosion

**Roswell, Georgia**(66, Male, USA) Anti-Muslim explosive terror plot

**Pendleton, Oregon**White supremacist explosion and shooting

**Austin, Texas**(49, Male, White, USA) White supremacist, anti-LGTBQ shooting

**New York City, New York** (28, Male, African American, USA) Anti-police shooting

## 2015

**Mesquite, Texas**(38, Male, Iraqi, Iraq and USA) Provided material support to ISIS, FSA

**Avondale, Arizona**(38 and 39, Males, Egyptian, USA) Provided material support to ISIL

**Topeka, Kansas**(21, Male, USA) Anti-military explosive terror plot for ISIL

**Augusta, Georgia**(37, Male, White, USA) Provided material and personnel support for ISIL

**Key West, Florida**(23, Male, USA) Explosive terror plot for ISIL

**Greentownship, Ohio**(21, Male, White, USA) Explosive terror plot for ISIS

**Chapel Hill, North Carolina**(42, Male, White, USA) Anti-Muslim shooting

**Kalamazoo, Michigan**(37, Male, White, USA) Anti-pornography arson

**St. Louis, Missouri**(Male, Bosnian, Bosnia) (25–26, Female, Bosnian Bosnia) (26–27, Male, Bosnian, Bosnia and USA) (Female, Bosnian, Bosnia) (38–39, Male, Bosnian, Bosnia (Female, Bosnian, Bosnia) Provided material support to and planned a terror plot for ISIL

**Manassas, Virginia**(17, Male, Sudanese, Sudan and USA) Provided material support to ISIL

**Reno, Nevada**\*No one was arrested for the incident\* Animal rights inspired arson

**Aurora, Illinois**(22, Male, USA) Provided personnel support to and planned a terror plot for ISIL

**Queens, New York**(28, Female, USA) (31, Female, Saudi, Saudi Arabia and USA) ISIL-inspired terror plot

**Topeka, Kansas**(29–30, Male, White, USA) Provided material support to ISIL

**Fort Lee, New Jersey**(21, Male, Jordanian, Jordan and USA) Provided personnel support to ISIL

**Fort Lee, New Jersey**(22, Male, Ghanaian, Ghana and USA) Provided personnel support to ISIL

**St. Paul, Minnesota**(19, Male, USA) Provided material and personnel support for ISIL

**Minneapolis, Minnesota**(20–21, Male, Somalian, USA) (18, Male, Somalian, USA) (20–21, Male, Kenyan, Kenya) (18, Male, Somalian, USA) (18, Male, Somalian, USA) (19, Male, Kenyan, Kenya and USA) Provided material support to ISIS

**Colorado Springs, Colorado** (40, Male, White, USA) Anti-government explosion

**Neptune, New Jersey**(46, Male, USA) Provided material and personnel support to ISIL

**Melbourne, Florida**\*No one was arrested for the incident\* Neo-Nazi inspired arson

**Kent, Ohio**\*No one was arrested for the incident\* Anti-government arson

**Brooklyn, New York**(24, Male, Uzbek, Uzbekistan) (19, Male, Kazakhstani, Kazakhstan) Provided material support to Al Qa'ida and ISIL

**Philadelphia, Pennsylvania**(30, Female, African American, USA) Provided personnel support to ISIL

**New Orleans, Louisiana**(59, Male, African American, USA) Armed assault

**San Diego, California**(24, Male, Syrian, Syria and USA) Provided personnel support to ISIL

**Santa Ana, California**(24, Male, USA) (24, Male, Sudan) Provided material and personnel support to ISIL

**Signal Mountain, Tennessee**(65, Male, White, USA) White supremacist terror plot

**Fort Lee, New Jersey**(23, Male, USA) Provided personnel support to ISIL

**Staten Island, New York**(20, Male, White, USA) Provided personnel support and planned a terror plot for ISIS

*(Continued)*

**Morgantown, North Carolina** (19, Male, White, USA) Provided personnel support to and planned a terror plot for ISIL
**Warwick, Rhode Island** (25, Male, USA) Planned a terror plot for ISIS
**Charleston, South Carolina** (21, Male, White, USA) White supremacist mass shooting
**Austin, Texas** (24, Male, White, USA) Provided personnel support to ISIS and al-Nusra Front
**Las Vegas, Nevada** (55, Male, White, USA) Planned an explosive terror plot inspired by racism and anti-government sentiments
**Knoxville, Tennessee** *No one was arrested for the incident* Arson
**Charlotte, North Carolina** *No one was arrested for the incident* Arson
**Houston, Texas** *No one was arrested for the incident* Arson
**Chattanooga, Tennessee** (20, Male, Palestinian-Jordanian, USA) Muslim extremist armed assault
**Miami, Florida** (45, Male, Cuban, Cuba) Planned a terror plot for ISIS
**Adams, Massachusetts** (23–24, Male, USA) Provided material and personnel support to, and planned a terror plot for ISIS

**Las Cruces, New Mexico** *No one was arrested for the incident* Explosion
**New Orleans, Louisiana** *No one was arrested for the incident* Anti-abortion arson
**Bullard, Texas** Rasheed Abdul Aziz (36, Male) Muslim extremist firearm threat

**Roseburg, Oregon** (26, Male, White, USA) White supremacist mass shooting
**Merced, California** (16, Male, USA) Muslim extremist armed assault

**Meriden, Connecticut** (44, Male, White, USA) Anti-Muslim armed assault
**Richmond, Virginia** (34, Male, White, USA) (33, Male, White, USA) (30, Male, White, USA) (58, Male, White, USA)

**Queens, New York** (19, Male, USA) Provided personnel support to and planned a terror plot for ISIS
**Roslindale, Massachusetts** (26, Male, USA) Planned a terror plot for ISIS
**Everett, Massachusetts** (25, Male, USA) Planned a terror plot for ISIS

**Sheffield Lake, Ohio** (39, Male, Bosnia and USA) Provided material support to ISIS
**Garland, Texas** (43, Male, USA) Provided material and personnel support to, and planned a terror plot for ISIL

**Macon, Georgia** *No one was arrested for the incident* Arson
**Gloverville, South Carolina** *No one was arrested for the incident* Arson
**Aurora, Illinois** *No one was arrested for the incident* Anti-abortion arson
**Lafayette, Louisiana** (59, Male, White, USA) White supremacist, neo-Nazi, and anti-LGBTQ mass shooting
**Lackawanna, New York** (44, Male, USA) Provided personnel support to ISIL
**Starkville, Mississippi** (20, Female, African American, USA) Muhammad Oda Dakhlalla (22, Male, USA) Provided personnel support to ISIS
**Las Cruces, New Mexico** *No one was arrested for the incident* Explosion
**Pullman, Washington** *No one was arrested for the incident* Anti-abortion arson
**Thousand Oaks, California** *No one was arrested for the incident* Anti-abortion arson

**Tupelo, Mississippi** (57, Male, White, USA) Right-wing extremist explosion
**Inglewood, California** (32, Male, White, USA) Anti-Muslim unarmed assault

**Falls Church, Virginia** (23, Male, White, USA) Anti-Muslim explosion
**Minneapolis, Minnesota** (23, Male, White, USA) (21, Male, White, USA)(26,

(52, Female, White, USA) White supremacist terror plot
**Minneapolis, Minnesota**\*No one was arrested for the incident\* White supremacist armed assault
**San Bernardino, California**(24, Male, Pakistani, USA) (25, Female, Pakistani, USA) Muslim extremist mass shooting
**Grand Forks, North Dakota**(21, Male, White, USA) Anti-Muslin arson
**Tracy, California**\*No one was arrested for the incident\* Anti-Muslim arson
**2016**
**Princeton, Oregon**Citizens for Constitutional Freedom (40, Male, White, USA) (43, Male, White, USA) (44, Male, White, USA) (59, Female, White, USA) (32, Male, White, USA) (45, Male, White, USA) (55, Male, White, USA) (34, Male, White, USA) (50, Male, White, USA) White supremacy, anti-government crime
**Dallas, Texas**(25, Male, African American, USA) Black separatist mass shooting
**Holliston, Massachusetts**(40, Male, White, USA) Anti-Muslim terror plot
**Manhattan, New York**(25, Male, Afghan, USA) Muslim extremist explosion
**Elizabeth, New Jersey**(25, Male, Afghan, USA) Muslim extremist explosion
**Garden City, Kansas**(49, Male, White, USA) (50, Male, White, USA) (46, Male, White, USA) White supremacist terror plot inspired by anti-government and anti-Muslim sentiments
**Indianapolis, Indiana**(20, Male, African American, USA) Anti-white shooting
**Reasnor, Iowa**\*No one was arrested for the incident\* Arson
**Century, Florida**\*No one was arrested for the incident\* Arson

Male, White, USA) (27, Male, White, USA) Racist, anti-government mass shooting
**Colorado Springs, Colorado**(57, Male, White, USA) Anti-abortion mass shooting
**Long Island City, New York**(51, Male, White, USA) Anti-Muslim unarmed assault
**Coachella, California**(19, Male, White, USA) Anti-Muslim arson

**Stockton, Utah**(57, Male, White, USA) Explosive terror plot inspired by anti-government and racist sentiments

**Baton Rouge, Louisiana**(29, Male, African American, USA) Shooting inspired by anti-government and black separatism
**Seaside Park, New Jersey**(25, Male, Afghan, USA) Muslim extremist explosion for ISIL
**St. Cloud, Minnesota**(19, Male, African American, USA) Muslim extremist shooting
**Kansas City, Missouri**\*No one was arrested for the incident\* Anti-Muslim arson
**Lincoln, Nebraska**\*No one was arrested for the incident\* Arson

**Storm Lake, Iowa**(35, Female, White, USA) (27, Female, White, USA) Environmentalist arson
**Hillsborough, North Carolina**\*No one was arrested for the incident\* Anti-Nazi, anti-Republican explosion
**Albuquerque, New Mexico**\*No one was arrested for the incident\* Pro-abortion arson

(Continued)

**Tacoma, Washington***No one was arrested for the incident* Arson

**Washington, District of Columbia** (27, Male, White, USA) Shooting

**Dallas, Texas**(29, Male, White, USA) Armed assault

**2017**

**Chicago, Illinois**(18, Male, African American, USA) (18, Female, African American, USA) (18, Male, African American, USA) (23, Female, African American, USA) Anti-Trump, anti-white hate crime

**Hudson Bend, Florida**\*No one was arrested for the incident* Anti-Muslim arson

**Bellevue, Washington**(37, Male) Arson

**Denver, Colorado**(37, Male, White, USA) Muslim extremist shooting

**Manchester, New Hampshire**\*No one was arrested for the incident* White supremacist arson

**Conway, South Carolina**(29, Male, White, USA)
White supremacist terror plot

**Olathe, Kansas**(51, Male, White, USA) White supremacist shooting

**Nome, North Dakota**\*No one was arrested for the incident* Arson

**Charlotte, North Carolina**(32, Male, African American, USA) Arson

**Vacaville, California**\*No one was arrested for the incident* White supremacist arson

**Lexington, Kentucky**(20, Male, White, USA) Right-wing extremist armed assault

**New York City, New York**(26, Male, USA) Anti-LGBTQ armed assault

**Bronx, New York**\*No one was arrested for the incident* Anti-Muslim shooting

**College Park, Maryland**(22, Male, White, USA) White supremacist stabbing

**Columbus, Ohio**(18, Male, Somali, Somalia and USA) Muslim extremist armed assault

**Redlands, California**\*No one was arrested for the incident* Arson

**Fort Lauderdale, Florida**(27, Male, Hispanic, USA) Muslim extremist mass shooting

**Fort Worth, Texas**\*No one was arrested for the incident* Arson

**Kansas City, Missouri**\*No one was arrested for the incident* Anti-LGBTQ armed assault

**Victoria, Texas**(25, Male, USA) White supremacist arson

**Thonotosassa, Florida**\*No one was arrested for the incident* Anti-Muslim arson

**Atlanta, Georgia**(27, Male, White, USA) White supremacy terror plot

**Kent, Washington**\*No one was arrested for the incident* Anti-Muslim shooting

**Chelsea, New York**(28, Male, White, USA) White supremacist stabbing

**Fresno, California**(39, Male, African American, USA) Anti-government, anti-white shooting

**Fairfield, California**(39, Male, White, USA) White supremacist arson

**Tampa, Florida**(18, Male, White, USA) Muslim extremist shooting and hostage situation

**Lexington, Kentucky**\*No one was arrested for the incident* Shooting

**Three Forks, Montana**(68, Male, White, USA) (38, Male, White, USA) (20, Male, White, USA) Anti-government, anti-police shooting

**Portland, Oregon**(35, Male, White, USA) White supremacist stabbing

**Alexandria, Virginia**(66, Male, White, USA) Anti-Republican mass shooting
**New York City, New York**\*No one was arrested for the incident\* Anti-Semitic arson
**Bronx, New York**(32, Male, African American, USA) Anti-police shooting
**Columbus, Indiana**\*No one was arrested for the incident\* Arson

**Campbelltown, Pennsylvania**\*No one was arrested for the incident\* Environmentalist arson
**Bloomington, Minnesota**\*No one was arrested for the incident\* Anti-Muslim explosion
**Oklahoma City, Oklahoma**(23, Male, White, USA) Anti-government explosive terror plot
**Baton Rouge, Louisiana**(24, Male, White, USA) White supremacist shooting
**Lincoln, Nebraska** (27, Male, White, USA) White supremacist terror plot
**Fletcher, North Carolina**(44, Male, White, USA) Explosive terror plot

**New York City, New York**(29, Male, Uzbek, Uzbekistan) Muslim extremist terror plot
**Champaign, Illinois**\*No one was arrested for the incident \* Anti-abortion explosive terror plot
**New York City, New York**(27, Male, Bangladeshi, Bangladesh) Muslim extremist explosive terror plot
**Jacksonville, Florida**(69, Male, Hispanic, USA) White supremacist terror plot
**Reston, Virginia**(17, Male, White, USA) Neo-Nazi shooting
**2018**
**Lake Forest, California**Samuel Woodward (20, Male, White, USA) White supremacist crime

**Flint, Michigan**(49, Male, Canadian, Canada) Muslim extremist stabbing
**Mount Vernon, Washington**(33, Male, White, USA) Right-wing extremist stabbing
**Dallas, Texas**\*No one was arrested for the incident\* Anti-LGBTQ arson
**Campbelltown, Pennsylvania**\*No one was arrested for the incident\* Environmentalist arson
**Kansas City, Missouri**\*No one was arrested for the incident\* Arson
**Houston, Texas**(25, Male, White, USA) Explosive terror plot
**Charlottesville, Virginia**(20, Male, White, USA) White supremacist crime
**Antioch, Tennessee**(25, Male, African American) Mass shooting
**Las Vegas, Nevada** (64, Male, White, USA) mass shooting
**Spokane, Washington**(32, Male, White, USA) (36, Male, White, USA) White supremacist hate crime
**Monroe, Louisiana**\*No one was arrested for the incident\* White supremacist arson

**Vale, North Carolina**\*No one was arrested for the incident\* Anti-LGBTQ arson
**Harrisburg, Pennsylvania**(51, Male) Muslim extremist shooting

**Aztech, New Mexico**(21, Male, White, USA) White supremacist shooting

**Denver, Colorado**(37, Male, USA) Right-wing extremist shooting

**Draffenville, Kentucky**Gabe Parker (16, Male, White, USA) Mass shooting

(Continued)

**Parkland, Florida**(19, Male, White, USA) Right-wing extremist mass shooting

**Austin, Texas**(23, Male, White, USA) Explosion

**Irvine, California**(26, Male, White, USA) White supremacist terror plot

**Nashville, Tennessee**(29, Male, White, USA) Mass shooting

**Santa Fe, Texas**(17, Male, White, USA) Mass shooting

**Annapolis, Maryland** Jarrod W. Ramos (38, Male, White, USA) Mass shooting

**Oakland, California**(27, Male, White, USA) White supremacist stabbing

**Cincinnati, Ohio**(29, Male, Hispanic, Puerto Rico) Mass shooting

**Miami, Florida** (56, Male, White, USA) White supremacist crime

**Tallahassee, Florida**(40, Male, White, USA) Misogynistic shooting

**Beaver Dam, Wisconsin**(28, Male, White, USA) White supremacist explosive terror plot

**Yountville, California**(36, Male, USA) Mass shooting

**San Bruno, California**(39, Female, Persian, Iran) Anti-censorship, anti-YouTube shooting

**Miami, Florida**(26, Male, White, USA) White supremacist terror plot

**Scottsdale, Arizona**(56, Male, African American, USA) Shooting

**Shawnee, Kansas** Ronald Lee Kidwell (47, Male, White, USA) White supremacist crime

**Jacksonville, Florida**(24, Male, White, USA) Mass shooting

**Louisville, Kentucky**(51, Male, White, USA) White supremacist shooting

**Pittsburg, Pennsylvania** (46, Male, White, USA) Anti-Semitic mass shooting

Sources: DOJ press releases, court filings, media reports (listed below).

*Biographical information includes: age, gender, race, and citizenship.

**Shootings constitute 3 or less shot, whereas mass shootings constitute 4 or more shot.

## Citations for Terror Map

"Abdurasul Hasanovich Juraboev." 2019. *Counter Extremism Project*, January 12. Accessed April 24, 2019. http://www.counterextremism.com/extremists/abdurasul-hasanovichjuraboev.

"Ahmed Mohammed El Gammal." 2018. *Counter Extremism Project*, May 23. Accessed May 1, 2019. http://www.counterextremism.com/extremists/ahmed-mohammed-el-gammal.

"Air Force Veteran Sentenced to 35 Years in Prison for Attempting to Join ISIS and Obstruction of Justice." 2017. *U.S. Department of Justice*, May 31. Accessed March 11, 2019. http://www.justice.gov/opa/pr/air-force-veteran-sentenced-35-years-prisonattempting-join-isis-and-obstruction-justice.

"Alaa Saadeh." 2018. *Counter Extremism Project*, May 24. Accessed March 11, 2019. https://www.counterextremism.com/extremists/alaa-saadeh.

"Alexander Ciccolo." 2018. *Counter Extremism Project*, September 17. Accessed April 23, 2019. http://www.counterextremism.com/extremists/alexander-ciccolo.

"Alexander E. Blair." 2017. *Counter Extremism Project*, January 17. Accessed April 23, 2019. http://www.counterextremism.com/extremists/alexander-e-blair.

Al Jazeera. 2016. "US Hands down Longest-ever Sentence for ISIL Support." *ISIS News*, March 18. Accessed March 4, 2019. http://www.aljazeera.com/news/2016/03/hands-longest-sentence-isil-support-160318054449490.html.

"Amir Said Abdul Rahman Al-Ghazi." 2018. *Counter Extremism Project*, May 23. Accessed April 11, 2019. http://www.counterextremism.com/extremists/amir-said-abdul-rahmanal-ghazi.

Andone, Dakin, and Keith Allen. 2018. "Alleged Shooter at Texas High School Spared People He Liked, Court Document Says." *CNN*, May 19. Accessed April 23, 2019. https://www.cnn.com/2018/05/18/us/texas-school-shooting/index.html.

"Arizona Man Indicted for Providing Material Support to Isil by Facilitating New York Man's Travel to Syria to Receive Terrorist Training." 2015. *U.S. Department of Justice*, August 27. Accessed February 21, 2019. https://www.justice.gov/usao-sdny/pr/arizona-man-indicted-providing-material-support-isil-facilitating-new-york-man-stravel.

"Arizona Man Sentenced to 30 Years for Conspiracy to Support ISIL and Other Federal Offenses." 2017. *U.S. Department of Justice*, February 8. Accessed April 11, 2019. http://www.justice.gov/opa/pr/arizona-man-sentenced-30-years-conspiracysupport-isil-and-other-federal-offenses.

"Armin Harcevic." 2017. *Counter Extremism Project*, January 12. Accessed April 24, 2019. http://www.counterextremism.com/extremists/armin-harcevic.

Astor, Maggie, and Maya Salam. 2018. "YouTube Shooting: Woman Wounds 3 Before Killing Herself, Police Say." *New York Times*, April 3. Accessed April 22, 2019. https://www.nytimes.com/2018/04/03/us/youtube-shooting.html.

Banks, Gabrielle, and Samantha Ketterer. 2018. "Houston Man Who Tried to Bomb Confederate Statue in Hermann Park Gets 6 Years in Federal Prison." *Houston Chronicle*, August 18. Accessed May 7, 2019. https://www.chron.com/news/houston-texas/houston/article/Man-who-tried-to-bomb-Confederate-statue-in-13162309.php.

Barker, Kim, Mosi Secret, and Richard Fausset. 2017. "Many Identities of New York Officers' Killer in a Life of Wrong Turns." *New York Times*, December 21. Accessed May 1, 2019. http://www.nytimes.com/2015/

01/03/nyregion/ismaaiyl-brinsleys-many-identities-fueled-life-of-wrong-turns.html.

Bidgood, Jess, and Dave Phillips. 2017. "Boston Terror Suspect's Shooting Highlights Concerns Over Reach of ISIS." *New York Times*, December 21. Accessed April 11, 2019. http://www.nytimes.com/2015/06/04/us/usaama-rahim-boston-terrorism-suspect-planned-beheading-authorities-say.html?hp&action=click&pgtype=Homepage&module=first-column-region®ion=top-news&WT.nav=top-news.

Bidgood, Jess, and Dave Philipps. 2015. "Portrait of Suspect in Boston Is Disputed." *New York Times*, June 5. Accessed April 11, 2019. https://www.nytimes.com/2015/06/05/us/portrait-of-boston-suspect-usaamah-rahim-is-disputed.html.

"Bilal Abood." 2018. *Counter Extremism Project*, May 22. Accessed May 1, 2019. http://www.counterextremism.com/extremists/bilal-abood.

"California Man Sentenced to 12 Years in Prison for Attempting to Join ISIL." 2016. *U.S. Department of Justice*, June 7. Accessed April 5, 2019. https://www.justice.gov/opa/pr/california-man-sentenced-12-years-prison-attempting-join-isil.

"The Cases." *Program on Extremism*. Accessed April 25, 2019. https://extremism.gwu.edu/cases.

"Cesar Altieri Sayoc Charged in 30-Count Indictment with Mailing Improvised Explosive Devices." 2018. *U.S. Department of Justice*, November 9. Accessed April 24, 2019. https://www.justice.gov/usao-sdny/pr/cesar-altieri-sayoc-charged-30-countindictment-mailing-improvised-explosive-devices.

"Chattanooga Man Sentenced for Solicitation to Burn Down a Mosque in Islamberg, New York." *U.S. Department of Justice*, October 3. Accessed April 8, 2019. http://www.justice.gov/opa/pr/chattanooga-man-sentenced-solicitation-burn-downmosque-islamberg-new-york.

"Chilling Coincidence? Tiny City Was Home to Two Attackers." 2016. NBC News. Accessed April 2, 2019. http://www.nbcnews.com/storyline/orlando-nightclub-massacre/omar-mateen-u-suicide-bomber-tied-fort-pierce-florida-n590846.

"Christopher Lee Cornell." 2017. *Counter Extremism Project*, May 18. Accessed April 24, 2019. http://www.counterextremism.com/extremists/christopher-lee-cornell.

"Colorado Woman Sentenced for Conspiracy to Provide Material Support to a Designated Foreign Terrorist Organization." 2016. *U.S. Department of Justice*, June 16. Accessed March 4, 2019. https://www.justice.

gov/opa/pr/colorado-woman-sentencedconspiracy-provide-material-support-designated-foreign-terrorist.

Culliton, Kathleen. 2017. "Umbrella Assault to be Investigated as Hate Crime, Police Say." *Brownsville-East New York, NY Patch*, June 2. Accessed May 6, 2019. https://patch.com/new-york/brownsville/umbrella-assault-be-investigated-hate-crime-police-say.

"David Daoud Wright." 2018. *Counter Extremism Project*, May 24. Accessed April 11, 2019. http://www.counterextremism.com/extremists/david-daoud-wright.

Ducharme, Jamie. 2018. "Austin Bombing Suspect Identified as Mark Anthony Conditt." *Time*, March 21. Accessed April 22, 2019. http://time.com/5207936/austin-texas-bombing-suspect-dead/.

"Esteban Santiago-Ruiz Sentenced to Life in Prison in Connection with Shooting at Fort Lauderdale-Hollywood International Airport." 2018. *U.S. Department of Justice*, August 17. Accessed May 2, 2019. https://www.justice.gov/usao-sdfl/pr/estebansantiago-ruiz-sentenced-life-prison-connection-shooting-fort-lauderdale.

"Fareed Mumini." 2017. *Counter Extremism Project*, January 12. Accessed April 11, 2019. http://www.counterextremism.com/extremists/fareed-mumini.

"Federal Charge Dropped against Man Accused of Sending Tweet That Set off Dallas Journalist's Seizure." 2017. *Dallas News*, November 28. Accessed April 25, 2019. https://www.dallasnews.com/news/courts/2017/11/27/prosecutors-drop-federal-chargeman-accused-sending-tweet-set-dallas-journalists-seizure.

"Federal Jury Convicts Man Who Attempted to Bomb Downtown Oklahoma City Bank." 2019. *U.S. Department of Justice*, February 26. Accessed May 7, 2019. https://www.justice.gov/usao-wdok/pr/federal-jury-convicts-man-who-attempted-bombdowntown-oklahoma-city-bank.

Field, Carla. 2017. "ISIS-supporting Teen Killed NC Neighbor, Planned Mass Murder, Feds Say." *WYFF*, October 9. Accessed April 10, 2019. http://www.wyff4.com/article/isis-supporting-teen-killed-nc-neighbor-planned-mass-murder-feds-say/7024054.

"Forsyth Deputy Shot, Suspect Dead, Courthouse Evacuated." 2014. *AJC*, June 9. Accessed April 5, 2019. http://www.ajc.com/news/forsyth-deputy-shot-suspect-dead-courthouseevacuated/ypNNTtXBbzUk7f3AYGzTmL/.

"Georgia Man Pleads Guilty to Attempting to Provide Material Support to ISIL." 2015. *U.S. Department of Justice*, May 27. Accessed April 04, 2019. http://www.justice.gov/opa/pr/georgia-man-pleads-guilty-attempting-provide-materialsupport-isil.

Gyan Jr., Joe. 2018. "Kenneth Gleason Won't Face Death Penalty in

September Slayings in Baton Rouge." *The Advocate*, July 11. Accessed May 7, 2019. https://www.theadvocate.com/baton_rouge/news/courts/article_7e17f080-8467-11e8-99cb-3b4ed3ebdb9e.html.

"Hamza Naj Ahmed." 2018. *Counter Extremism Project*, May 22. Accessed April 29, 2019. http://www.counterextremism.com/extremists/hamza-naj-ahmed.

"Hamza Naj Ahmed Indicted for Conspiring to Provide Material Support to the Islamic State of Iraq and the Levant." 2015. *Federal Bureau of Investigation*, February 19. Accessed April 29, 2019. https://www.fbi.gov/contact-us/field-offices/minneapolis/news/press-releases/hamza-naj-ahmed-indicted-for-conspiring-to-provide-material-support-to-the-islamic-state-of-iraq-and-the-levant.

"Harlem Suarez." 2018. *Counter Extremism Project*, May 24. Accessed April 10, 2019. http://www.counterextremism.com/extremists/harlem-suarez.

"Hasan Rasheed Edmonds." 2018. *Counter Extremism Project*, May 23. Accessed April 23, 2019. http://www.counterextremism.com/extremists/hasan-rasheed-edmonds.

Hauser, Christine, and Julia Jacobs. 2018. "Cincinnati Gunman Kills Three and Is Fatally Shot by Police." *New York Times*, September 6. Accessed April 24, 2019. https://www.nytimes.com/2018/09/06/us/cincinnati-shooting.html.

"Holliston Man Sentenced for Unlawful Possession of Ammunition." 2017. *U.S. Department of Justice*, October 12. Accessed April 18, 2019. https://www.justice.gov/usao-ma/pr/holliston-man-sentenced-unlawful-possessionammunition.

"Incident Summary for GTDID: 201403180089." *Global Terrorism Database*. Accessed April 4, 2019. https://www.start.umd.edu/gtd/search/IncidentSummary.aspx?gtdid=201403180089.

"Incident Summary for GTDID: 201403250090." *Global Terrorism Database*. Accessed April 4, 2019. https://www.start.umd.edu/gtd/search/IncidentSummary.aspx?gtdid=201403250090.

"Incident Summary for GTDID: 201404120086." *Global Terrorism Database*. Accessed April 2, 2019. http://www.start.umd.edu/gtd/search/IncidentSummary.aspx?gtdid=201404120086.

"Incident Suamrry for GTDID: 201404270057." *Global Terrorism Database*. Accessed April 2, 2019. http://www.start.umd.edu/gtd/search/IncidentSummary.aspx?gtdid=201404270057.

"Incident Summary for GTDID: 201405050073." *Global Terrorism Database*. Accessed April 3, 2019. http://www.start.umd.edu/gtd/search/IncidentSummary.aspx?gtdid=201405050073.

"Incident Summary for GTDID: 201406060065." *Global Terrorism Database*. Accessed April 3, 2019. http://www.start.umd.edu/gtd/search/IncidentSummary.aspx?gtdid=201406060065.

"Incident Summary for GTDID: 201406110089." *Global Terrorism Database.* Accessed April 5, 2019. http://www.start.umd.edu/gtd/search/IncidentSummary.aspx?gtdid=201406110089.

"Incident Summary for GTDID: 201406250082." *Global Terrorism Database.* Accessed April 5, 2019. http://www.start.umd.edu/gtd/search/IncidentSummary.aspx?gtdid=201406250082.

"Incident Summary for GTDID: 201409110001." *Global Terrorism Database.* Accessed April 8, 2019. http://www.start.umd.edu/gtd/search/IncidentSummary.aspx?gtdid=201409110001.

"Incident Summary for GTDID: 201409120032." *Global Terrorism Database.* Accessed April 25, 2019. http://www.start.umd.edu/gtd/search/IncidentSummary.aspx?gtdid=201409120032.

"Incident Summary for GTDID: 201410030065." *Global Terrorism Database.* Accessed April 25, 2019. http://www.start.umd.edu/gtd/search/IncidentSummary.aspx?gtdid=201410030065.

"Incident Summary for GTDID: 201410230047." *Global Terrorism Database.* Accessed April 25, 2019. http://www.start.umd.edu/gtd/search/IncidentSummary.aspx?gtdid=201410230047.

"Incident Summary for GTDID: 201410240071." *Global Terrorism Database.* Accessed April 25, 2019. http://www.start.umd.edu/gtd/search/IncidentSummary.aspx?gtdid=201410240071.

"Incident Summary for GTDID: 201411040086." *Global Terrorism Database.* Accessed April 25, 2019. http://www.start.umd.edu/gtd/search/IncidentSummary.aspx?gtdid=201411040086.

"Incident Summary for GTDID: 201411040087." *Global Terrorism Database.* Accessed April 25, 2019. http://www.start.umd.edu/gtd/search/IncidentSummary.aspx?gtdid=201411040087.

"Incident Summary for GTDID: 201411230072." *Global Terrorism Database.* Accessed April 25, 2019. http://www.start.umd.edu/gtd/search/IncidentSummary.aspx?gtdid=201411230072.

"Incident Summary for GTDID: 201412070129." *Global Terrorism Database.* Accessed April 25, 2019. http://www.start.umd.edu/gtd/search/IncidentSummary.aspx?gtdid=201412070129.

"Incident Summary for GTDID: 201412200060." *Global Terrorism Database.* Accessed April 25, 2019. http://www.start.umd.edu/gtd/search/IncidentSummary.aspx?gtdid=201412200060.

"Incident Summary for GTDID: 201501060024." *Global Terrorism Database.* Accessed April 25, 2019. http://www.start.umd.edu/gtd/search/IncidentSummary.aspx?gtdid=201501060024.

"Incident Summary for GTDID: 201502100004." *Global Terrorism Database.* Accessed April 25, 2019. http://www.start.umd.edu/gtd/search/IncidentSummary.aspx?gtdid=201502100004.

"Incident Summary for GTDID: 201502170127." *Global Terrorism Database*. Accessed April 25, 2019. http://www.start.umd.edu/gtd/search/IncidentSummary.aspx?gtdid=201502170127.

"Incident Summary for GTDID: 201502180067." *Global Terrorism Database*. Accessed April 25, 2019. http://www.start.umd.edu/gtd/search/IncidentSummary.aspx?gtdid=201502180067.

"Incident Summary for GTDID: 201502230104." *Global Terrorism Database*. Accessed April 25, 2019. http://www.start.umd.edu/gtd/search/IncidentSummary.aspx?gtdid=201502230104.

"Incident Summary for GTDID: 201503100045." *Global Terrorism Database*. Accessed April 25, 2019. http://www.start.umd.edu/gtd/search/IncidentSummary.aspx?gtdid=201503100045.

"Incident Summary for GTDID: 201503200036." *Global Terrorism Database*. Accessed April 25, 2019. http://www.start.umd.edu/gtd/search/IncidentSummary.aspx?gtdid=201503200036.

"Incident Summary for GTDID: 201506220069." *Global Terrorism Database*. Accessed April 25, 2019. http://www.start.umd.edu/gtd/search/IncidentSummary.aspx?gtdid=201506220069.

"Incident Summary for GTDID: 201506230056." *Global Terrorism Database*. Accessed April 25, 2019. http://www.start.umd.edu/gtd/search/IncidentSummary.aspx?gtdid=201506230056.

"Incident Summary for GTDID: 201506240051." *Global Terrorism Database*. Accessed April 25, 2019. http://www.start.umd.edu/gtd/search/IncidentSummary.aspx?gtdid=201506240051.

"Incident Summary for GTDID: 201506260046." *Global Terrorism Database*. Accessed April 25, 2019. http://www.start.umd.edu/gtd/search/IncidentSummary.aspx?gtdid=201506260046.

"Incident Summary for GTDID: 201507150077." *Global Terrorism Database*. Accessed April 25, 2019. http://www.start.umd.edu/gtd/search/IncidentSummary.aspx?gtdid=201507150077.

"Incident Summary for GTDID: 201507160062." *Global Terrorism Database*. Accessed April 25, 2019. http://www.start.umd.edu/gtd/search/IncidentSummary.aspx?gtdid=201507160062.

"Incident Summary for GTDID: 201507190097." *Global Terrorism Database*. Accessed April 25, 2019. http://www.start.umd.edu/gtd/search/IncidentSummary.aspx?gtdid=201507190097.

"Incident Summary for GTDID: 201508010105." *Global Terrorism Database*. Accessed April 25, 2019. http://www.start.umd.edu/gtd/search/IncidentSummary.aspx?gtdid=201508010105.

"Incident Summary for GTDID: 201508020115." *Global Terrorism Database*. Accessed April 25, 2019. http://www.start.umd.edu/gtd/search/IncidentSummary.aspx?gtdid=201508020115.

"Incident Summary for GTDID: 201508140093." *Global Terrorism Database*. Accessed April 25, 2019. http://www.start.umd.edu/gtd/search/IncidentSummary.aspx?gtdid=201508140093.

"Incident Summary for GTDID: 201509040048." *Global Terrorism Database*. Accessed April 25, 2019. http://www.start.umd.edu/gtd/search/IncidentSummary.aspx?gtdid=201509040048.

"Incident Summary for GTDID: 201509130079." *Global Terrorism Database*. Accessed April 25, 2019. http://www.start.umd.edu/gtd/search/IncidentSummary.aspx?gtdid=201509130079.

"Incident Summary for GTDID: 201509300082." *Global Terrorism Database*. Accessed April 25, 2019. https://www.start.umd.edu/gtd/search/IncidentSummary.aspx?gtdid=201509300082.

"Incident Summary for GTDID: 201511010076." *Global Terrorism Database*. Accessed April 25, 2019. https://www.start.umd.edu/gtd/search/IncidentSummary.aspx?gtdid=201511010076.

"Incident Summary for GTDID: 201511040056." *Global Terrorism Database*. Accessed April 25, 2019. https://www.start.umd.edu/gtd/search/IncidentSummary.aspx?gtdid=201511040056.

"Incident Summary for GTDID: 201511150043." *Global Terrorism Database*. Accessed April 25, 2019. http://www.start.umd.edu/gtd/search/IncidentSummary.aspx?gtdid=201511150043.

"Incident Summary for GTDID: 201511190054." *Global Terrorism Database*. Accessed April 25, 2019. https://www.start.umd.edu/gtd/search/IncidentSummary.aspx?gtdid=201511190054.

"Incident Summary for GTDID: 201511230084." *Global Terrorism Database*. Accessed April 25, 2019. https://www.start.umd.edu/gtd/search/IncidentSummary.aspx?gtdid=201511230084.

"Incident Summary for GTDID: 201512020012." *Global Terrorism Database*. Accessed April 25, 2019. https://www.start.umd.edu/gtd/search/IncidentSummary.aspx?gtdid=201512020012.

"Incident Summary for GTDID: 201512020012." *Global Terrorism Database*. Accessed April 25, 2019. https://www.start.umd.edu/gtd/search/IncidentSummary.aspx?gtdid=201512020012.

"Incident Summary for GTDID: 201512050031." *Global Terrorism Database*. Accessed April 25, 2019. https://www.start.umd.edu/gtd/search/IncidentSummary.aspx?gtdid=201512050031.

"Incident Summary for GTDID: 201512080038." *Global Terrorism Database*. Accessed April 25, 2019. https://www.start.umd.edu/gtd/search/IncidentSummary.aspx?gtdid=201512080038.

"Incident Summary for GTDID: 201512110031." *Global Terrorism Database*. Accessed April 25, 2019. https://www.start.umd.edu/gtd/search/IncidentSummary.aspx?gtdid=201512110031.

"Incident Summary for GTDID: 201512260016." *Global Terrorism Database*. Accessed April 25, 2019. https://www.start.umd.edu/gtd/search/IncidentSummary.aspx?gtdid=201512260016.

"Incident Summary for GTDID: 201609170001." *Global Terrorism Database*. Accessed April 25, 2019. https://www.start.umd.edu/gtd/search/IncidentSummary.aspx?gtdid=201609170001.

"Incident Summary for GTDID: 201609170002." *Global Terrorism Database*. Accessed April 25, 2019. https://www.start.umd.edu/gtd/search/IncidentSummary.aspx?gtdid=201609170002.

"Incident Summary for GTDID: 201609170004." *Global Terrorism Database*. Accessed April 25, 2019. https://www.start.umd.edu/gtd/search/IncidentSummary.aspx?gtdid=201609170004.

"Incident Summary for GTDID: 201609180001." *Global Terrorism Database*. Accessed April 25, 2019. https://www.start.umd.edu/gtd/search/IncidentSummary.aspx?gtdid=201609180001.

"Incident Summary for GTDID: 201609240025." *Global Terrorism Database*. Accessed April 25, 2019. https://www.start.umd.edu/gtd/search/IncidentSummary.aspx?gtdid=201609240025.

"Incident Summary for GTDID: 201610030040." *Global Terrorism Database*. Accessed April 25, 2019. https://www.start.umd.edu/gtd/search/IncidentSummary.aspx?gtdid=201610030040.

"Incident Summary for GTDID: 201610040058." *Global Terrorism Database*. Accessed April 25, 2019. https://www.start.umd.edu/gtd/search/IncidentSummary.aspx?gtdid=201610040058.

"Incident Summary for GTDID: 201610090043." *Global Terrorism Database*. Accessed April 25, 2019. https://www.start.umd.edu/gtd/search/IncidentSummary.aspx?gtdid=201610090043.

"Incident Summary for GTDID: 201610150013." *Global Terrorism Database*. Accessed April 25, 2019. https://www.start.umd.edu/gtd/search/IncidentSummary.aspx?gtdid=201610150013.

"Incident Summary for GTDID: 201610160022." *Global Terrorism Database*. Accessed April 25, 2019. https://www.start.umd.edu/gtd/search/IncidentSummary.aspx?gtdid=201610160022.

"Incident Summary for GTDID: 201611080059." *Global Terrorism Database*. Accessed April 25, 2019. https://www.start.umd.edu/gtd/search/IncidentSummary.aspx?gtdid=201611080059.

"Incident Summary for GTDID: 201611230062." *Global Terrorism Database*. Accessed April 25, 2019. https://www.start.umd.edu/gtd/search/IncidentSummary.aspx?gtdid=201611230062.

"Incident Summary for GTDID: 201611250026." *Global Terrorism Database*. Accessed April 25, 2019. https://www.start.umd.edu/gtd/search/IncidentSummary.aspx?gtdid=201611250026.

"Incident Summary for GTDID: 201611280001." *Global Terrorism Database.* Accessed April 25, 2019. https://www.start.umd.edu/gtd/search/IncidentSummary.aspx?gtdid=201611280001.

"Incident Summary for GTDID: 201612040047." *Global Terrorism Database.* Accessed April 25, 2019. https://www.start.umd.edu/gtd/search/IncidentSummary.aspx?gtdid=201612040047.

"Incident Summary for GTDID: 201612080038." *Global Terrorism Database.* Accessed April 25, 2019. https://www.start.umd.edu/gtd/search/IncidentSummary.aspx?gtdid=201612080038.

"Incident Summary for GTDID: 201612150044." *Global Terrorism Database.* Accessed April 25, 2019. https://www.start.umd.edu/gtd/search/IncidentSummary.aspx?gtdid=201612150044.

"Incident Summary for GTDID: 201701020076." *Global Terrorism Database.* Accessed May 2, 2019. https://www.start.umd.edu/gtd/search/IncidentSummary.aspx?gtdid=201701020076.

"Incident Summary for GTDID: 201701060022." *Global Terrorism Database.* Accessed May 2, 2019. https://www.start.umd.edu/gtd/search/IncidentSummary.aspx?gtdid=201701060022.

"Incident Summary for GTDID: 201701070015." *Global Terrorism Database.* Accessed May 2, 2019. https://www.start.umd.edu/gtd/search/IncidentSummary.aspx?gtdid=201701070015.

"Incident Summary for GTDID: 201701070022." *Global Terrorism Database.* Accessed May 2, 2019. https://www.start.umd.edu/gtd/search/IncidentSummary.aspx?gtdid=201701070022.

"Incident Summary for GTDID: 201701140040." *Global Terrorism Database.* Accessed May 2, 2019. https://www.start.umd.edu/gtd/search/IncidentSummary.aspx?gtdid=201701140040.

"Incident Summary for GTDID: 201701200055." *Global Terrorism Database.* Accessed May 2, 2019. https://www.start.umd.edu/gtd/search/IncidentSummary.aspx?gtdid=201701200055.

"Incident Summary for GTDID: 201701310059." *Global Terrorism Database.* Accessed May 2, 2019. https://www.start.umd.edu/gtd/search/IncidentSummary.aspx?gtdid=201701310059.

"Incident Summary for GTDID: 201702060025." *Global Terrorism Database.* Accessed May 2, 2019. https://www.start.umd.edu/gtd/search/IncidentSummary.aspx?gtdid=201702060025.

"Incident Summary for GTDID: 201702100037." *Global Terrorism Database.* Accessed May 2, 2019. https://www.start.umd.edu/gtd/search/IncidentSummary.aspx?gtdid=201702100037.

"Incident Summary for GTDID: 201702240020." *Global Terrorism Database.* Accessed May 2, 2019. https://www.start.umd.edu/gtd/search/IncidentSummary.aspx?gtdid=201702240020.

"Incident Summary for GTDID: 201703030012." *Global Terrorism Database.* Accessed May 2, 2019. https://www.start.umd.edu/gtd/search/IncidentSummary.aspx?gtdid=201703030012.

"Incident Summary for GTDID: 201703220053." *Global Terrorism Database.* Accessed May 2, 2019. https://www.start.umd.edu/gtd/search/IncidentSummary.aspx?gtdid=201703220053.

"Incident Summary for GTDID: 201704060031." *Global Terrorism Database.* Accessed May 2, 2019. https://www.start.umd.edu/gtd/search/IncidentSummary.aspx?gtdid=201704060031.

"Incident Summary for GTDID: 201704130023." *Global Terrorism Database.* Accessed May 2, 2019. https://www.start.umd.edu/gtd/search/IncidentSummary.aspx?gtdid=201704130023.

"Incident Summary for GTDID: 201704180060." *Global Terrorism Database.* Accessed May 2, 2019. https://www.start.umd.edu/gtd/search/IncidentSummary.aspx?gtdid=201704180060.

"Incident Summary for GTDID: 201704240032." *Global Terrorism Database.* Accessed May 6, 2019. https://www.start.umd.edu/gtd/search/IncidentSummary.aspx?gtdid=201704240032.

"Incident Summary for GTDID: 201704270028." *Global Terrorism Database.* Accessed May 6, 2019. https://www.start.umd.edu/gtd/search/IncidentSummary.aspx?gtdid=201704270028.

"Incident Summary for GTDID: 201704270029." *Global Terrorism Database.* Accessed May 6, 2019. https://www.start.umd.edu/gtd/search/IncidentSummary.aspx?gtdid=201704270029.

"Incident Summary for GTDID: 201704280023." *Global Terrorism Database.* Accessed May 6, 2019. https://www.start.umd.edu/gtd/search/IncidentSummary.aspx?gtdid=201704280023.

"Incident Summary for GTDID: 201704280029." *Global Terrorism Database.* Accessed May 6, 2019. https://www.start.umd.edu/gtd/search/IncidentSummary.aspx?gtdid=201704280029.

"Incident Summary for GTDID: 201705190057." *Global Terrorism Database.* Accessed May 6, 2019. https://www.start.umd.edu/gtd/search/IncidentSummary.aspx?gtdid=201705190057.

"Incident Summary for GTDID: 201705190058." *Global Terrorism Database.* Accessed May 6, 2019. https://www.start.umd.edu/gtd/search/IncidentSummary.aspx?gtdid=201705190058.

"Incident Summary for GTDID: 201705260036." *Global Terrorism Database.* Accessed May 6, 2019. https://www.start.umd.edu/gtd/search/IncidentSummary.aspx?gtdid=201705260036.

"Incident Summary for GTDID: 201705290065." *Global Terrorism Database.* Accessed May 6, 2019. https://www.start.umd.edu/gtd/search/IncidentSummary.aspx?gtdid=201705290065.

"Incident Summary for GTDID: 201705300053." *Global Terrorism Database*. Accessed May 7, 2019. https://www.start.umd.edu/gtd/search/IncidentSummary.aspx?gtdid=20170530053.
"Incident Summary for GTDID: 201706140029." *Global Terrorism Database*. Accessed May 6, 2019. https://www.start.umd.edu/gtd/search/IncidentSummary.aspx?gtdid=201706140029.
"Incident Summary for GTDID: 201706210022." *Global Terrorism Database*. Accessed May 6, 2019. https://www.start.umd.edu/gtd/search/IncidentSummary.aspx?gtdid=201706210022.
"Incident Summary for GTDID: 201706260019." *Global Terrorism Database*. Accessed May 6, 2019. https://www.start.umd.edu/gtd/search/IncidentSummary.aspx?gtdid=201706260019.
"Incident Summary for GTDID: 201707050048." *Global Terrorism Database*. Accessed May 6, 2019. https://www.start.umd.edu/gtd/search/IncidentSummary.aspx?gtdid=201707050048.
"Incident Summary for GTDID: 201707070026." *Global Terrorism Database*. Accessed May 6, 2019. https://www.start.umd.edu/gtd/search/IncidentSummary.aspx?gtdid=201707070026.
"Incident Summary for GTDID: 201707080029." *Global Terrorism Database*. Accessed May 7, 2019. https://www.start.umd.edu/gtd/search/IncidentSummary.aspx?gtdid=201707080029.
"Incident Summary for GTDID: 201707090044." *Global Terrorism Database*. Accessed May 7, 2019. https://www.start.umd.edu/gtd/search/IncidentSummary.aspx?gtdid=201707090044.
"Incident Summary for GTDID: 201707130061." *Global Terrorism Database*. Accessed May 7, 2019. https://www.start.umd.edu/gtd/search/IncidentSummary.aspx?gtdid=201707130061.
"Incident Summary for GTDID: 201708040042." *Global Terrorism Database*. Accessed May 7, 2019. https://www.start.umd.edu/gtd/search/IncidentSummary.aspx?gtdid=201708040042.
"Incident Summary for GTDID: 201708050005." *Global Terrorism Database*. Accessed May 7, 2019. https://www.start.umd.edu/gtd/search/IncidentSummary.aspx?gtdid=201708050005.
"Incident Summary for GTDID: 201708190026." *Global Terrorism Database*. Accessed May 7, 2019. https://www.start.umd.edu/gtd/search/IncidentSummary.aspx?gtdid=201708190026.
"Incident Summary for GTDID: 201709110044." *Global Terrorism Database*. Accessed May 7, 2019. https://www.start.umd.edu/gtd/search/IncidentSummary.aspx?gtdid=201709110044.
"Incident Summary for GTDID: 201709120031." *Global Terrorism Database*. Accessed May 7, 2019. https://www.start.umd.edu/gtd/search/IncidentSummary.aspx?gtdid=201709120031.

"Incident Summary for GTDID: 201709140041." *Global Terrorism Database*. Accessed May 7, 2019. https://www.start.umd.edu/gtd/search/IncidentSummary.aspx?gtdid=201709140041.

"Incident Summary for GTDID: 201709240018." *Global Terrorism Database*. Accessed May 7, 2019. https://www.start.umd.edu/gtd/search/IncidentSummary.aspx?gtdid=201709240018.

"Incident Summary for GTDID: 201710010018." *Global Terrorism Database*. Accessed May 7, 2019. https://www.start.umd.edu/gtd/search/IncidentSummary.aspx?gtdid=201710010018.

"Incident Summary for GTDID: 201710060013." *Global Terrorism Database*. Accessed May 7, 2019. https://www.start.umd.edu/gtd/search/IncidentSummary.aspx?gtdid=201710060013.

"Incident Summary for GTDID: 201710080028." *Global Terrorism Database*. Accessed May 7, 2019. https://www.start.umd.edu/gtd/search/IncidentSummary.aspx?gtdid=201710080028.

"Incident Summary for GTDID: 201710310017." *Global Terrorism Database*. Accessed May 7, 2019. https://www.start.umd.edu/gtd/search/IncidentSummary.aspx?gtdid=201710310017.

"Incident Summary for GTDID: 201710310042." *Global Terrorism Database*. Accessed May 7, 2019. https://www.start.umd.edu/gtd/search/IncidentSummary.aspx?gtdid=201710310042.

"Incident Summary for GTDID: 201711070054." *Global Terrorism Database*. Accessed May 8, 2019. https://www.start.umd.edu/gtd/search/IncidentSummary.aspx?gtdid=201711070054.

"Incident Summary for GTDID: 201711130042." *Global Terrorism Database*. Accessed May 8, 2019. https://www.start.umd.edu/gtd/search/IncidentSummary.aspx?gtdid=201711130042.

"Incident Summary for GTDID: 201712110001." *Global Terrorism Database*. Accessed May 8, 2019. https://www.start.umd.edu/gtd/search/IncidentSummary.aspx?gtdid=201712110001.

"Incident Summary for GTDID: 201712220022." *Global Terrorism Database*. Accessed May 8, 2019. https://www.start.umd.edu/gtd/search/IncidentSummary.aspx?gtdid=201712220022.

"Incident Summary for GTDID: 201712220023." *Global Terrorism Database*. Accessed May 8, 2019. https://www.start.umd.edu/gtd/search/IncidentSummary.aspx?gtdid=201712220023.

"Jasminka Ramic." 2017. *Counter Extremism Project*, January 12. Accessed April 24, 2019. http://www.counterextremism.com/extremists/jasminka-ramic.

"John T. Booker." 2018. *Counter Extremism Project*, May 23. Accessed May 1, 2019. https://www.counterextremism.com/extremists/john-t-booker.

"Jonas Marcel Edmonds." 2017. *Counter Extremism Project*, May 26.

Accessed April 23, 2019. http://www.counterextremism.com/extremists/jonas-marcel-edmonds.

"Joshua Ray Van Haften." 2018. *Counter Extremism Project*, May 24. Accessed April 4, 2019. http://www.counterextremism.com/extremists/joshua-ray-van-haften.

Joyner, Chris. 2018. "Ricin Charges Dropped against Georgia White Supremacist." *AJC*, October 3. Accessed April 18, 2019. https://www.ajc.com/news/crime--law/ricin-charges-dropped-against-georgia-white-supremacist/0GWcj07MLSMvcthfnApsWM/.

"Jury Convicts Texas Man of Hate Crime in the Burning of Victoria, Texas, Mosque." 2919. *U.S. Department of Justice*, March 27. Accessed April 18, 2019. https://www.justice.gov/opa/pr/jury-convicts-texas-man-hate-crime-burning-victoriatexas-mosque.

"Kansas Man Pleads Guilty to Hate Crime and Firearm Offenses in Shooting of Two Indian Nationals and Third Man at a Bar." 2018. *U.S. Department of Justice*, May 21. Accessed April 18, 2019. https://www.justice.gov/opa/pr/kansas-man-pleads-guilty-hate-crime-and-firearm-offenses-shooting-two-indian-nationals-and.

"Katy Man Charged with Multiple Crimes, Including Possession of Explosive Materials." 2014. *Federal Bureau of Investigation*, March 28. Accessed April 1, 2019. https://archives.fbi.gov/archives/houston/press-releases/2014/katy-man-charged-withmultiple-crimes-including-possession-of-explosive-materials.

"Keebler Pleads Guilty to Attempted Destruction of Federal Property by Use of an Explosive." 2018. *U.S. Department of Justice*, April 30. Accessed April 18, 2019. https://www.justice.gov/usao-ut/pr/keebler-pleads-guilty-attempted-destructionfederal-property-use-explosive.

"Keonna Thomas." 2017. *Trial and Terror—The Intercept*, April 17. Accessed April 4, 2019. https://trial-and-terror.theintercept.com/people/058e2c18-eb4e-4ca5-a092-c12f790aa574.

"Keonna Thomas." 2019. *Counter Extremism Project*, February 20. Accessed April 4, 2019. http://www.counterextremism.com/extremists/keonna-thomas.

Kim, Victoria, and Joseph Serna. 2018. "Gunman, Three Hostages Found Dead at Yountville Veterans Facility: 'These Brave Women' Killed." *Los Angeles Times*, March 10. Accessed April 22, 2019. https://www.latimes.com/local/lanow/la-me-veterans-hostages-20180309-story.html.

Kocher, Greg. 2018. "'I Apologize for My Actions.' Machete Attacker Is Sentenced for Transylvania Attack." *Kentucky*, December 16. Accessed May 6, 2019. https://www.kentucky.com/news/local/crime/article223103120.html.

"Leon Nathan Davis." 2017. *Counter Extremism Project*, January 12, 2017. Accessed April 04, 2019. http://www.counterextremism.com/extremists/leon-nathan-davis.

Levenson, Eric, and AnneClaire Stapleton. 2018. "Two Killed in Shooting at Jacksonville Video Game Tournament." *CNN*, August 27. Accessed April 24, 2019. https://edition.cnn.com/2018/08/26/us/jacksonville-madden-shooting/index.html.

Loller, Travis, and Jonathan Mattise. 2019. "Emanuel Kidega Samson." *AP News*, May 29. Accessed May 7, 2019. https://www.apnews.com/EmanuelKidegaSamson.

"Man Sentenced for Leaving Pipe Bomb at Vickery Creek Park." 2016. *U.S. Department of Justice*, February 9. Accessed May 1, 2019. http://www.justice.gov/usaondga/pr/man-sentenced-leaving-pipe-bomb-vickery-creek-park.

"Manassas Man Pleads Guilty to Providing Material Support to ISIL." 2015. *U.S. Department of Justice*, June 11. Accessed April 11, 2019. https://www.justice.gov/usao-edva/pr/manassas-man-pleads-guilty-providing-materialsupport-isil.

McCoy, Terrence. 2014. "How Douglas McAuthur McCain Became the First American to Die Fighting for the Islamic State." *Washington Post*, August 27. Accessed April 8, 2019. http://www.washingtonpost.com/news/morning-mix/wp/2014/08/27/how-douglas-mcarthur-mccain-became-the-first-american-to-die-fighting-for-the-islamic-state/?noredirect=on&utm_term=.419fe1027062.

"Mediha Salkicevic." 2017. *Counter Extremism Project*, January 12. Accessed April 24, 2019. http://www.counterextremism.com/extremists/mediha-salkicevic.

"Miami Resident and Isil Sympathizer Sentenced to 10 Years in Prison for Illegally Possessing a Firearm." 2016. *U.S. Department of Justice*, February 4. Accessed April 24, 2019. http://www.justice.gov/usao-sdfl/pr/miami-resident-and-isil-sympathizer-sentenced-10-years-prison-illegally-possessing.

"Mississippi Couple Charged with Conspiracy and Attempt to Provide Material Support to ISIL." 2015. *U.S. Department of Justice*, August 14. Accessed April 25, 2019. http://www.justice.gov/opa/pr/mississippi-couple-charged-conspiracy-and-attempt-provide-material-support-isil.

"Mohamad Saeed Kodaimati." 2017. *Counter Extremism Project*, January 12, 2017. Accessed April 23, 2019. http://www.counterextremism.com/extremists/mohamad-saeed-kodaimati.

"Mohamed Abdihamid Farah." 2018. *Counter Extremism Project*, May 23. Accessed April 10, 2019. http://www.counterextremism.com/extremists/mohamed-abdihamid-farah.

"Mohammed Hamzah Khan." Counter Extremism Project. January 12, 2017. Accessed April 8, 2019. http://www.counterextremism.com/extremists/mohammed-hamzah-khan.

"Muhammad Dakhlalla." 2018. *Counter Extremism Project*, May 23. Accessed April 25, 2019. http://www.counterextremism.com/extremists/muhammad-dakhlalla.

"Muhanad Badawi." 2018. *Counter Extremism Project*, May 23. Accessed April 11, 2019.http://www.counterextremism.com/extremists/muhanad-badawi.

"Munther Omar Saleh." 2018. *Counter Extremism Project*, May 24. Accessed April 11, 2019.http://www.counterextremism.com/extremists/munther-omar-saleh.

"Nevada County Man Sentenced to Nearly 30 Years in Prison for Wounding Two Law Enforcement Officers in Gun Battle." 2015. *U.S. Department of Justice*, August 28. Accessed April 5, 2019. http://www.justice.gov/usao-edca/pr/nevada-county-man-sentenced-nearly-30-years-prison-wounding-two-law-enforcement.

"New York Man Sentenced to 18 Years for ISIS-Directed Terrorist Attacks in New York City." 2018. *U.S. Department of Justice*, February 06. Accessed April 11, 2019. https://www.justice.gov/opa/pr/new-york-man-sentenced-18-years-isis-directed-terrorist-attacks-new-york-city.

"Nicholas Alexander Rovinski." 2018. *Counter Extremism Project*, May 24. Accessed April 11, 2019. http://www.counterextremism.com/extremists/nicholas-alexander-rovinski. "Nihad Rosic." 2017. *Counter Extremism Project*, January 12. Accessed April 24, 2019. http://www.counterextremism.com/extremists/nihad-rosic.

"North Carolina Man Charged with Attempting to Provide Material Support to ISIL and Weapon Offenses." 2015. *U.S. Department of Justice*, June 22. Accessed April 10, 2019. http://www.justice.gov/opa/pr/north-carolina-man-charged-attempting-provide-material-support-isil-and-weapon-offenses.

"North Carolina Man Sentenced to Serve 243 Months in Prison for Attempting to Provide Material Support to a Designated Foreign Terrorist Organization." 2015. *U.S. Department of Justice*, May 13. Accessed April 8, 2019. http://www.justice.gov/opa/pr/north-carolina-man-sentenced-serve-243-months-prison-attempting-provide-material-support.

"Ohio Man Charged with Federal Hate Crimes Related to August 2017 Rally in Charlottesville." 2019. *U.S. Department of Justice*, March 27. Accessed April 22, 2019. https://www.justice.gov/opa/pr/ohio-man-charged-federal-hate-crimes-related-august-2017-rally-charlottesville.

"Ohio Man Sentenced to 16 Years in Prison for Providing Support to ISIS, Being a Felon in Possession of Firearms." 2018. *U.S. Department of*

*Justice,* June 20. Accessed April 11, 2019. http://www.justice.gov/opa/pr/ohio-man-sentenced-16-years-prison-providing-support-isis-being-felon-possession-firearms.

"Orange County, California, Man Charged in New Indictment with Attempting to Provide Material Support to ISIL." 2016. *U.S. Department of Justice,* June 16. Accessed April 8, 2019. http://www.justice.gov/opa/pr/orange-county-california-man-charged-new-indictment-attempting-provide-material-support-isil.

Park, Madison. 2018. "BART Stabbing Suspect Charged with Murder." *CNN,* July 27. Accessed April 23, 2019. https://www.cnn.com/2018/07/25/us/bart-stabbing-suspect-murder-charge/index.html.

"Pennsylvania Man Charged with Federal Hate Crimes for Tree of Life Synagogue Shooting." 2018. *U.S. Department of Justice,* November 5. Accessed April 22, 2019. https://www.justice.gov/opa/pr/pennsylvania-man-charged-federal-hate-crimes-tree-life-synagogue-shooting.

Perez, Evan. 2018. "What We Know about Dimitrios Pagourtzis, the Alleged Santa Fe High School Shooter." *CNN,* May 21. Accessed April 23, 2019. https://www.cnn.com/2018/05/18/us/dimitrios-pagourtzis-santa-fe-suspect/index.html.

Petroski, William. 2018. "A Year Later, Still No Federal Charges against 'Saboteurs' of Dakota Access Pipeline. Why?" *Des Moines Register,* July 23. Accessed April 25, 2019. https://www.desmoinesregister.com/story/news/politics/2018/07/23/dakota-access-pipeline-iowa-sabotage-no-federal-charges-jessica-reznicek-ruby-montoya/801287002/.

"Philadelphia Woman Arrested for Attempting to Provide Material Support to ISIL." 2016. *U.S. Department of Justice,* June 15. Accessed April 4, 2019. http://www.justice.gov/opa/pr/philadelphia-woman-arrested-attempting-provide-material-support-isil.

"'Pizzagate' Gunman Sentenced to Four Years in Prison." June 22, 2017. *NBCNews.com,* Accessed April 25, 2019. https://www.nbcnews.com/news/us-news/pizzagate-gunman-edgar-maddison-welch-sentenced-four-years-prison-n775621.

"Raleigh Man Pleads Guilty to Conspiring to Provide Material Support for Terrorism." 2016. *U.S. Department of Justice,* January 8. Accessed February 28, 2019. https://www.justice.gov/opa/pr/raleigh-man-pleads-guilty-conspiring-provide-material-support-terrorism.

"Raleigh Men Sentenced for Conspiracy to Provide Material Support to Terrorist." 2016. *U.S. Department of Justice,* July 5. Accessed April 3, 2019. http://www.justice.gov/usao-ednc/pr/raleigh-men-sentenced-conspiracy-provide-material-support-terrorist.

"Ramiz Zijad Hodzic." 2018. *Counter Extremism Project,* May 23. Accessed

April 24, 2019. http://www.counterextremism.com/extremists/ramiz-zijad-hodzic.

Ransom, Jan. 2019. "White Supremacist Who Killed Black Man to Incite Race War Sentenced to Life in Prison." *New York Times*, February 13. Accessed April 18, 2019. https://www.nytimes.com/2019/02/13/nyregion/james-harris-jackson-timothy-caughman.html.

Reese, Diana. 2015. "Jury Recommends Death Penalty for White Supremacist Frazier Glenn Miller." *Washington Post*, September 8. Accessed April 2, 2019. http://www.washingtonpost.com/news/post-nation/wp/2015/09/08/white-supremacist-frazier-glenn-miller-sentenced-to-die/?utm_term=.45ebe0f81e08.

Reese, Diana. 2015. "The Strange Trial of the Avowed Anti-Semite and White Supremacist Charged in the Kansas City JCC Killings." *Washington Post*, August 27. Accessed April 2, 2019. http://www.washingtonpost.com/news/post-nation/wp/2015/08/27/the-strange-trial-of-the-avowed-anti-semite-and-white-supremacist-charged-in-the-kansas-city-jcc-killings/?utm_term=.d552297cfb2d.

"Rhode Island Man Sentenced for Conspiring to Commit Acts of Terrorism to Support ISIS." 2017. *U.S. Department of Justice*, December 20. Accessed April 11, 2019. http://www.justice.gov/usao-ma/pr/rhode-island-man-sentenced-conspiring-commit-acts-terrorism-support-isis.

"Rochester Man Indicted on Charges of Attempting to Provide Material Support to ISIS, Attempting to Kill U.S. Soldiers and Possession of Firearms and Silencers." 2014. *U.S. Department of Justice*, September 18. Accessed March 4, 2019. http://www.justice.gov/nsd/pr/rochester-man-indicted-charges-attempting-provide-material-support-isis-attempting-kill-us.

"Round Rock Man Pleads Guilty to Attempting to Provide Material Support to Terrorists." 2014. *U.S. Department of Justice*, December 16. Accessed April 4, 2019. https://www.justice.gov/usao-wdtx/pr/round-rock-man-pleads-guilty-attempting-provide-material-support-terrorists.

"Samy El-Goarany." 2018. *Counter Extremism Project*, May 23. Accessed May 1, 2019. http://www.counterextremism.com/extremists/samy-el-goarany.

Schwirtz, Michael, and William Rashbaum. 2018. "Attacker With Hatchet Is Said to Have Grown Radical on His Own." *New York Times*, January 19. Accessed May 1, 2019. http://www.nytimes.com/2014/10/25/nyregion/man-who-attacked-police-with-hatchet-ranted-about-us-officials-say.html.

"Sedina Unkic Hodzic." 2017. *Counter Extremism Project*, January 12.

Accessed April 24, 2019. https://www.counterextremism.com/extremists/sedina-unkic-hodzic.

Serna, Joseph, Hailey Branson-Potts, and James Queally. 2017. "Suspect in Fresno Shooting Rampage Spoke about Racial Conflict and Black Nationalism." *Los Angeles Times*, April 18. Accessed May 2, 2019. https://www.latimes.com/local/lanow/la-me-fresno-shooter-suspect-20170418-story.html.

Smith, John L. 2017. "Nevada Rancher Cliven Bundy Goes on Trial for Leading 2014 Armed..." *Reuters*, October 30. Accessed April 2, 2019. http://www.reuters.com/article/us-nevada-militia/nevada-rancher-cliven-bundy-goes-on-trial-for-leading-2014-armed-standoff-idUSKBN1CZ0Y7.

Smith, Mitch, and Monica Davey. 2017. "4 Black Suspects Charged in Videotaped Beating of White Teenager in Chicago." *New York Times*, January 5. Accessed May 2, 2019. https://www.nytimes.com/2017/01/05/us/chicago-racially-charged-attack-video.html.

Stevens, Matt, and Matthew Haag. 2018. "Arizona Man Left a Trail of 6 Bodies, Police Believe, Then Added His Own." *New York Times*, June 4. Accessed April 23, 2019. https://www.nytimes.com/2018/06/04/us/jonbenet-ramsey-psychiatrist-killed.html.

Strom, Kevin J., John S. Hollywood, and Mark Pope. 2015. "Terrorist Plots against the United States: What We Have Really Faced, and How We Might Best Defend against It." *RAND Homeland Security and Defense Center*. https://www.rand.org/pubs/working_papers/WR1113.html

"Suspect Charged with Arson of Immigrant-owned Store to Appear in Court." *NBCNews.com*. Accessed May 2, 2019. https://www.nbcnews.com/news/asian-america/suspect-alleged-arson-immigrant-owned-store-appear-court-n745051.

"Suspect in Montana Deputy Killing Appears Intrigued with Antigovernment Fringe." *Southern Poverty Law Center*. Accessed April 18, 2019. https://www.splcenter.org/hatewatch/2017/05/17/suspect-montana-deputy-killing-appears-intrigued-antigovernment-fringe.

Temple-Raston, Dina. 2014. "ISIS Used Predatory Tools and Tactics to Convince U.S. Teens to Join." *NPR*, December 11. Accessed April 11, 2019. https://www.npr.org/2014/12/11/370022514/isis-used-predatory-tools-and-tactics-to-convince-u-s-teens-to-join.

Temple-Raston, Dina. 2015. "New York Man Accused Of Plotting To Explode Pressure Cooker Bombs." *NPR*, June 17. Accessed April 2, 2019. http://www.npr.org/sections/thetwo-way/2015/06/16/415060978/new-york-man-accused-of-plotting-to-explode-pressure-cooker-bombs.

"Terror from the Right." 2014. *Southern Poverty Law Center*. Accessed April 10, 2019. https://www.splcenter.org/20180723/terror-right#2014.

"Terror from the Right." 2015. *Southern Poverty Law Center*. Accessed April 8, 2019. http://www.splcenter.org/20180723/terror-right#2015.

"Terror from the Right." 2016. *Southern Poverty Law Center*. Accessed April 18, 2019. https://www.splcenter.org/20180723/terror-right#2016.

"Terror from the Right." 2017. *Southern Poverty Law Center*. Accessed April 18, 2019. https://www.splcenter.org/20180723/terror-right#2017.

"Terror from the Right." 2018. *Southern Poverty Law Center*. Accessed April 18, 2019. https://www.splcenter.org/20180723/terror-right#2018.

"Texas Man Sentenced to 82 Months in Prison for Attempting to Travel to Syria to Join ISIL." 2015. *U.S. Department of Justice*, June 5. Accessed April 11, 2019. http://www.justice.gov/opa/pr/texas-man-sentenced-82-months-prison-attempting-travel-syria-join-isil.

"Three Southwest Kansas Men Sentenced to Prison for Plotting to Bomb Somali Immigrants in Garden City." 2019. *U.S. Department of Justice*, June 4. Accessed April 25, 2019. https://www.justice.gov/opa/pr/three-southwest-kansas-men-sentenced-prison-plotting-bomb-somali-immigrants-garden-city.

"Two Minnesotans Charged With Conspiracy to Provide Material Support to the Islamic State of Iraq and the Levant." 2015. *U.S. Department of Justice*, April 30. Accessed April 3, 2019. http://www.justice.gov/usao-mn/pr/two-minnesotans-charged-conspiracy-provide-material-support-islamic-state-iraq-and-levant.

"Two Orange County Men Arrested on Federal Charges of Conspiring to Provide Material Support to ISIL." 2015. *U.S. Department of Justice*, June 23. Accessed April 11, 2019. http://www.justice.gov/usao-cdca/pr/two-orange-county-men-arrested-federal-charges-conspiring-provide-material-support-isil.

"Two Queens, New York, Residents Charged with Conspiracy to Use a Weapon of Mass Destruction." 2016. *U.S. Department of Justice*, June 16. Accessed April 4, 2019. http://www.justice.gov/opa/pr/two-queens-new-york-residents-charged-conspiracy-use-weapon-mass-destruction.

"U.S. Army National Guard Soldier and His Cousin Indicted for Conspiring to Support Terrorism." 2016. *U.S. Department of Justice*, June 15. Accessed April 23, 2019. http://www.justice.gov/opa/pr/us-army-national-guard-soldier-and-his-cousin-indicted-conspiring-support-terrorism.

"A U.S. Teen's Turn to Radicalism, and the Safety Net That Failed." 2019. *Reuters*, June 6. Accessed April 11, 2020. http://www.reuters.com/investigates/special-report/usaextremists-teen/.

United States of America v. Abdullahi Yusuf and Abdi Nur (United States District Court for the District of Minnesota November 24, 2014). Affidavit of special agent John Thomas.

United States of America v. Abdurasul Hasanovich Juraboev (aka "Abdulloh Ibn Hasan"), Akhror Saidakhmetov, Abror Habibov, and Dilkhayot Kasimov (United States District Court Eastern District of New York April 6, 2015). Superseding Indictment.

United States of America v. Abdurasul Hasanovich Juraboev (aka "Abdulloh Ibn Hasan"), Akhror Saidakhmetov, and Abror Habibov (United States District Court Eastern District of New York February 24, 2015). Complaint and Affidavit in Support of Arrest Warrant.

United States of America v. Alaa Saadeh (United States District Court District of New Jersey June 26, 2015). Affidavit of Suzanne Walsh.

United States of America v. Alexander Ciccolo (United States District Court for the District of Massachusetts July 4, 2015). Affidavit of special agent Jeffrey Lawrence.

United States of America v. Alexander E. Blair (United States District Court District of Kansas April 10, 2015).

"United States of America v. Arafat Nagi." *ICD–United States of America v. Arafat Nagi–Asser Institute.* Accessed April 23, 2019. http://www.internationalcrimesdatabase.org/Case/3303/United-States-of-America-v-Arafat-Nagi/.

United States of America v. Arafat M. Nagi (United States District Court for the Western District of New York July 28, 2015). Affidavit of special agent Amanda Pike.

United States of America v. Bilal Abood (United States District Court Northern District of Texas May 13, 2015). Affidavit of an unnamed FBI special agent.

United States of America v. Christopher Cornell (aka Raheel Mahrus Ubaydah) (United States District Court for the Southern District of Ohio Western Division May 7, 2015). Superseding Indictment.

United States of America v. Fareed Mumuni (United States District Court Eastern District of New York June 17, 2015). Affidavit of special agent Christopher Buscaglia.

United States of America v. Harlem Suarez (aka Almiak Benitez) (United States District Court for the Southern District of Florida July 28, 2015). Affidavit of special agent Brian Thomas Wade.

United States of America v. John T. Booker, Jr. (aka "Mohammed Abdullah Hassan") (United States District Court District of Kansas April 10, 2015).

United States of America v. Joshua Van Haften (United States District Court for the Western District of Wisconsin October 28, 2014). Affidavit of special agent Eric Roehl. United States of America v. Keonna Thomas (aka Fatayat Al Khilafah and YoungLioness) (United States District Court for the Eastern District of Pennsylvania April 3, 2015). Criminal Complaint.

United States of America v. Mohamad Saeed Kodaimati (United States District Court Southern District of California April 23, 2015). Affidavit of special agent David Cotter in support of criminal complaint and arrest warrant.

United States of America v. Mohamed Abdihamid Farah, Adnan Abdihamid Farah, Abdurahman Yasin Daud, Zacharia Yusuf Abdurahman, Hanad Mustafe Musse, Guled Ali Omar (United States District Court for the District of Minnesota April, 2015). Affidavit of special agent Nicholas Marshall.

United States of America v. Mohammed Hamzah Khan (United States District Court Northern District of Illinois Eastern Division October 6, 2014). Affidavit of special agent Dana McNeal.

United States of America v. Munther Omar Saleh (aka Abu Omar al-Ramli and Abu Omar ar- Ramli) (United States District Court Eastern District of New York June 13, 2015). Affidavit of special agent Christopher Buscaglia.

United States of America v. Nader Saadeh (United States District Court District of New Jersey August 1, 2015). Affidavit of special agent Suzanne Walsh.

United States of America v. Nicholas Michael Teausant (United States District Court for the Eastern District of California March 17, 2014). Affidavit of special agent Justin Jacobs.

United States of America v. Noelle Velentzas and Asia Siddiqui (aka Najma Samaa and Murdiyyah) (United States District Court Eastern District of New York April 1, 2015). Affidavit of special agent Nicholas Hanak.

United States of America v. Ramiz Zijad Hodzic (aka Siki Ramiz Hodzic), Sedina Unkic Hodzic, Nihad Rosic (aka Yahya AbuAyesha Mudzahid), Mediha Medy Salkicevic (aka Medy Ummuluna and Bosna Mexico), Armin Harcevic, and Jasminka Ramic (United States District Court Eastern District of Missouri Eastern Division February 5, 2015).

United States of America v. Samuel Rahamin Topaz (United States District Court District of New Jersey June 18, 2015). Affidavit of special agent Suzanne Walsh.

United States of America v. Tairod Nathan Webster Pugh (United States District Court Eastern District of New York March 6, 2015). Grand Jury Indictment.

"Usaamah Abdullah Rahim." 2018. *Counter Extremism Project*, January 22. Accessed April 11, 2019. http://www.counterextremism.com/extremists/usaamah-abdullah-rahim.

"Virginia Man Sentenced to More than 11 Years for Providing Material Support to ISIL." 2015. *U.S. Department of Justice*, August 28. Accessed April 11, 2019. http://www.justice.gov/opa/pr/virginia-man-sentenced-more-11-years-providing-material-support-isil.

"Virginia Woman Sentenced for Making False Statements in an International Terrorism Investigation." 2015. *U.S. Department of Justice*, May 11. Accessed April 11, 2019. http://www.justice.gov/opa/pr/virginia-woman-sentenced-making-false-statements-international-terrorism-investigation.

White, Ed. 2019. "Canadian Sentenced to Life in Prison for US Airport Attack." *AP News*, April 18. Accessed May 6, 2019. https://www.apnews.com/5dff30b7a1804f07b3799bb814a22bdd.

"White Supremacist Pleads Guilty to Federal Gun Charges." 2018. *U.S. Department of Justice*, February 28. Accessed April 18, 2019. https://www.justice.gov/usao-sc/pr/white-supremacist-pleads-guilty-federal-gun-charges.

Williams, Timothy, and Amy Harmon. 2018. "Maryland Shooting Suspect Had Long-Running Dispute With Newspaper." *New York Times*, June 29. Accessed April 23, 2019. https://www.nytimes.com/2018/06/29/us/jarrod-ramos-annapolis-shooting.html.

"Wisconsin Man Sentenced to 10 Years in Prison for Attempting to Provide Material Support to ISIL." 2017. *U.S. Department of Justice*, February 17. Accessed April 4, 2019. http://www.justice.gov/opa/pr/wisconsin-man-sentenced-10-years-prison-attempting-provide-material-support-isil.

Yan, Holly. 2018. "Who Is New York Terror Suspect Sayfullo Saipov?" *CNN*, November 2. Accessed May 7, 2019. https://www.cnn.com/2017/11/01/us/sayfullo-saipov-new-york-attack/index.html.

Yan, Holly, AnneClaire Stapleton, and Paul P. Murphy. 2018. "Kentucky School Shooting: 2 Students Killed, 18 Injured." *CNN*, January 24. Accessed May 22, 2019. https://www.cnn.com/2018/01/23/us/kentucky-high-school-shooting/index.html.

# 3 Mass Shootings

In this chapter, we explore America's gun problem and proposals by survivors and advocacy groups for gun control measures. We review government's response to gun violence and find that the public is largely dissatisfied with policymaking aimed at curbing violence. The lack of policy solutions to reduce violence has led to increasing reliance on training the public to learn to live with and survive violent attacks. We look at the public's experience with active shooter training and first aid for shooting victims. The chapter also addresses mass shootings in schools. Relying on original data from the Chapman Survey of American Fears (CSAF), we identify attitudes towards school safety and beliefs about the prevalence of violence in schools, as well as the media's role in heightening fears. Finally, we examine the public's responses to school shootings and policies advocated by the students, faculty, and community members.

Fear of being the victim of a mass shooting is the fastest-growing fear in America. In the year 2019 alone, there were 417 mass shootings, the highest number ever seen in the United States, see Figure 3.1.[1] The nation reeled from the violence that never seemed to end that summer. On a Saturday afternoon in August, in El Paso, Texas, 23 people died and 25 were wounded in a mass shooting at a busy Walmart. Among the dead were Jordan and Andre Anchondo, who died shielding their baby son from the gunfire.[2] The gunman had opened fire with an assault weapon he had purchased over the Internet from Romania and had picked up at a local gun store.[3] The 21-year-old shooter, a white male, planned the attack to target Latinos. He had driven from Allen, Texas, where he lived with his grandparents, to El Paso in order to carry out his attack because he thought he would be able to kill Mexican immigrants.[4] He uploaded a manifesto to the Internet during the shooting. It said, "This attack is a response to the Hispanic invasion of Texas. They are the instigators, not me. I am simply defending my country from cultural and ethnic replacement brought on by the invasion."[5] The manifesto referred to the massacre

54  Mass Shootings

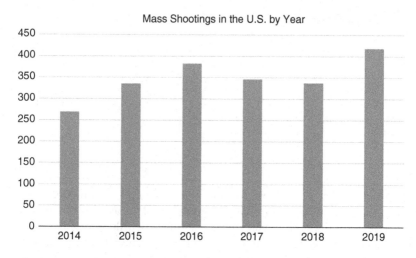

*Figure 3.1* Mass Shootings in the United States by Year.
Source: Everytown for Gun Safety, https://everytownresearch.org/massshootingsreports/mass-shootings-in-america-2009-2019/.

of Muslims in a mass shooting in Christ Church, New Zealand. The attack ended when the shooter surrendered to authorities. He was charged with 90 federal charges, including hate crimes.[6]

The day after the El Paso shooting, Dayton, Ohio saw the deaths of 9 people and 27 wounded by a 24-year-old gunman. He used an AR-15 assault weapon to open fire on people in the crowded Oregon District, which is filled with bars and restaurants. The attack lasted just 32 seconds before the gunman was killed by police. Earlier that summer, on July 28, 2019, at the Gilroy Garlic Festival in California, 3 people were killed and 20 wounded when a shooter wielding an AK-47 assault weapon opened fire on families at the festival, shooting 36 rounds.[7] Among the dead were two children. The violence ended when police officers returned fire, wounding him, and the shooter took his own life.[8]

It is no wonder that fear of mass or random shootings has skyrocketed since 2016, where 26.9% of Americans were afraid or very afraid, to 47.2% of Americans in 2019, see Figure 3.2.

Even as fears rise in response to mass shootings, so to do gun sales. One study looked at the increase in gun sales in California, following mass shootings in Newtown, Connecticut, and San Bernardino, California. They find that purchases increase by 53% after Newtown and 41% after San Bernardino. In addition, the increase in sales was higher among residents

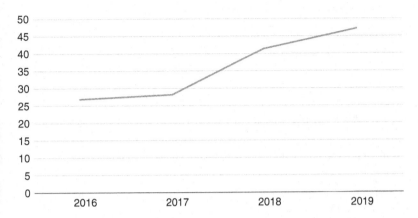

*Figure 3.2* Fear of Mass Shootings in the United States by Year.
Source: Chapman Survey of American Fears, Waves 3–6.

in the San Bernardino area, compared with the rest of California.[9] Another study found that, "… shootings that receive a high amount of media coverage are more likely to be associated with significant increases in handgun purchasing and shootings with more fatalities are more likely to be associated with significant decreases in handgun purchasing."[10] The CSAF found that media usage patterns did increase the likelihood of buying a gun out of fear. In particular, those who heavily rely on social media for news, are more likely to report buying a gun out of fear. We also find that fans of TV crime dramas are 2.41 times more likely to purchase a gun out of fear than those who never watch such shows. Paranormal program viewers are 2.58 times more likely to buy a gun when compared to those who never watch these shows. The impact of media usage remains statistically significant, even when we control for the effects of partisanship, ideology, and sex, see Table 3.1. The relationship between fear of crime and media usage has been well documented,[11] so it is not surprising that these viewing patterns are also associated with the purchase of firearms as well. In Table 3.1, we can also see that men are 2.61 times more likely to purchase a gun out of fear than women, Republicans are 1.85 times more likely to purchase a gun out of fear than a Democrat, and conservatives are 2.18 times more likely to purchase a gun out of fear than liberals.

Scholars have identified the main causes of an increase in gun sales following a mass shooting as fear or anxiety over being the victim in such a shooting (amplified by press coverage), and fear that the government will enact gun control laws that restrict the purchase of firearms and

Table 3.1 Buying a Gun Out of Fear by Media Use

| Variables | B | Exp(B) |
|---|---|---|
| Conservative | .78* | 2.18 |
| Moderate | .61 | 1.84 |
| Republican | .62* | 1.85 |
| Independent | .34 | 1.41 |
| Male | .96*** | 2.61 |
| Read a local newspaper every day | .66 | 1.93 |
| Read a national newspaper every day | .08 | 1.08 |
| Watch the national nightly network news every day | .20 | 1.22 |
| Watch Fox News every day | −.41 | .66 |
| Watch CNN every day | .53 | 1.70 |
| Watch MSNBC every day | −.34 | .71 |
| Watch TV news (such as PBS, BBC) every day | −.88 | .42 |
| Watch local TV news every day | .30 | 1.35 |
| Listen to talk radio every day | .29 | 1.34 |
| Read online news websites every day | .05 | 1.05 |
| Get news from social media such as Twitter every day | .93* | 2.54 |
| Read news magazine such as *Time* or *Newsweek* every day | .68 | 1.97 |
| Watch daytime talk shows very often | −.41 | .78 |
| Watch comedy news shows such as *The Daily Show* very often | −.08 | .93 |
| Watch TV crime dramas such as *CSI* and *Law & Order* very often | .88* | 2.41 |
| Watch TV true crime shows such as *Dateline NBC* very often | −.09 | .91 |
| Watch science fiction, fantasy, superheroes, vampires, zombies movies, or TV shows very often | .12 | .74 |
| Watch paranormal TV and/or movies very often | .95* | 2.58 |
| **Model Stats** | | |
| Constant | −4.67 | |
| N | 1400 | |
| Cox & Snell R Square | .10 | |
| Nagelkerke R Square | .21 | |
| Dependent Variable: "Purchased a gun" because of respondent's fears. | | |

Source: 2015 CSAF **p < .001; **p < .01; *p < .05 (two-tailed tests).

ammunition. Each of these causes will be examined here in turn. First, anxiety about safety can lead some gun purchasers to believe that arming themselves will provide a measure of protection in the event of another shooting. Other sources of mass anxiety and upheaval lead to an increase in gun purchases as well. For example, following the 9/11 attacks, there was a modest increase in gun sales, though press reports made it sound greater than it was.[12]

Even the COVID-19 pandemic led to an increase in gun sales. As the virus swept across the globe, Americans began to hoard a number of commodities, leading to widespread shortages of toilet paper, sanitizing wipes, and bleach. They also purchased guns in record numbers. In March of 2020, the FBI processed 2.4 million background checks for gun purchases, a higher number than at any point in the previous 20 years.[13] In April 2020, sales continued to make records, as 2.9 million background checks were performed.[14] Many gun stores defied shelter-in-place orders and press reports often pictured long lines of people waiting to buy guns and ammunition.[15] At the City Arms store in northern California, one man who was waiting in line told reporters, "The government is trying to do everything it can to keep society intact. But if society is unraveling, it's up to us to protect ourselves ... "[16] Gun stores remained open across the country, despite many governors closing them—along with other businesses—to slow the rate of coronavirus infections. Nevertheless, gun stores in states such as Massachusetts, Michigan, New Mexico, New York, and Washington remained open for business.[17] The Department of Homeland Security had published guidelines for what kinds of businesses were considered essential and should remain open during the pandemic. These businesses included pharmacies, groceries, and in a move that shocked many, gun stores and gun manufacturers.[18] Members of Congress were outraged at the inclusion of guns in the DHS guidelines. For example, Democratic Representative Debbie Wasserman Schultz (FL-23) said:

> No reputable public health expert would urge local leaders to add more firearms to a mix of public anxiety and the swelling economic and mental health stress that this global pandemic has ushered in. It is an absurd and dangerous idea that only a gun lobby could hatch ... We need to make our communities safer. This essential business advisory does the opposite. We cannot shoot this virus. Defeating COVID-19 requires bolstering our health systems and diligent social distancing and sanitation measures. The National Rifle Association already unleashed a gun violence health menace on this nation, we should not allow gun lobbyists to make this unfolding viral health pandemic any worse.[19]

Nevertheless, the Trump Administration persisted in designating gun stores to be essential businesses. In addition to the DHS guidance, Trump spurred on gun sales with his tweets. For example, as protestors pushed back against governors who issued stay-at-home orders, Trump fanned the flames by tweeting, "LIBERATE VIRGINIA, and save your great 2nd Amendment. It is under siege!"[20] Soaring gun sales, and the increase in background checks they necessitated, led the Justice Department, under Attorney General Bill Barr, to request an increase in funding. In particular, they needed more personnel for the National Instant Criminal Background

Check System (NICS) and for the Bureau of Alcohol, Tobacco, Firearms and Explosives (ATF) because they are charged with the responsibility of seizing guns from those who have failed background checks. Gun laws are such that a delay in returning the results of a background check can result in someone who ought not own a gun, purchasing it anyway.

Many background checks just take minutes. But some can take much longer. And if a background check is still under way and unresolved after three days, the gun buyer can take the weapon home. That's when things can get complicated; if the NICS system concludes that someone has taken a weapon home who shouldn't have been able to, then agents from ATF have to go retrieve it.[21]

Unfortunately, the increase in gun purchases during the pandemic also led to an increase in gun violence as well, leading to 776 deaths and injuries over a 3-month period, in excess of what would have been expected without the surge in gun purchases.[22]

In addition to fear and anxiety over highly publicized shootings, or events that are out of one's control, like a pandemic, concern that the government will restrict access to guns and ammunition fuels much of the buying. Gun sales increased during the 2008 election, as an Obama win was widely regarded as a harbinger of stricter gun control regulation. Sadly, those states that had the greatest increase in gun purchases "were 20% more likely to experience a shooting event where at least three people were killed."[23] The study attributes this to having a greater number of guns in circulation. As noted earlier, mass shootings are often accompanied by an uptick in gun purchases, as the National Rifle Association and other 2nd Amendment advocates warn that gun control legislation is likely to pass as a reaction to the killings.

Following mass shootings, the NRA issues statements that blame the cause of the shooting on multiple things—but never guns. Following the killing of nine parishioners at the Emanual African Methodist Episcopal Church in Charleston, South Carolina, by a 21-year-old white supremacist, the NRA blamed one of the victims for the attack. In a bizarre statement, they reasoned that Pastor George C. Pickney was to blame for the murders, "He voted against concealed-carry … Eight of his church members who might be alive if he had expressly allowed members to carry handguns in church are dead. Innocent people died because of his position on a political issue."[24] This appalling statement, far from being aberration, is actually quite representative of the NRA's response after any mass shooting. For example, following the heart wrenching killing of 26 people—20 of whom were children—at Sandy Hook Elementary School, the NRA issued a statement that blamed a variety of factors from "unwillingness" to prosecute criminals to video games and movies. As usual, they were attempting to short-circuit efforts by lawmakers, gun control advocates, and especially the families of the victims to bring about meaningful gun control reforms:

> So now, due to a declining willingness to prosecute dangerous criminals, violent crime is increasing again for the first time in 19 years! Add another hurricane, terrorist attack or some other natural or man-made disaster, and you've got a recipe for a national nightmare of violence and victimization.
> And here's another dirty little truth that the media try their best to conceal: There exists in this country a callous, corrupt and corrupting shadow industry that sells, and sows, violence against its own people. Through vicious, violent video games with names like Bulletstorm, Grand Theft Auto, Mortal Kombat and Splatterhouse. And here's one: it's called Kindergarten Killers. It's been online for 10 years. How come my research department could find it and all of yours either couldn't or didn't want anyone to know you had found it?
> Then there's the blood-soaked slasher films like "American Psycho" and "Natural Born Killers" that are aired like propaganda loops on "Splatterdays" and every day, and a thousand music videos that portray life as a joke and murder as a way of life. And then they have the nerve to call it "entertainment."[25]

The statement goes on to rail about the ineffectiveness of gun control measures and makes the oft-quoted statement, "The only thing that stops a bad guy with a gun is a good guy with a gun."[26] Since those remarks about Sandy Hook, that sentiment has been echoed many times. For example, following the murder of six people in the Tree of Life Synagogue in Pittsburgh, President Trump said:

> If they had protection inside, the results would have been far better," Trump said hours after the shooting Saturday. "This is a dispute that will always exist, I suspect, but if they had some kind of a protection inside the temple, maybe this would have been a very different situation. They didn't and [the shooter] was unfortunately able to do things he shouldn't have been able to do.[27]

The notion that carrying a firearm will prevent an assault and that enacting so-called right to carry laws would have prevented killings, as the NRA and gun control opponents routinely suggest, has been debunked by carefully conducted empirical studies.[28] Indeed, "More than 30 peer-reviewed studies, focusing on individuals as well as populations, have been published that confirm ... that guns are associated with an increased risk for violence and homicide ..."[29] One such study found that states that adopted right to carry laws see "... 13 to 15% higher aggregate violent crime rates 10 years after adoption."[30] Even though scientific studies have rendered the NRA position—that more guns are needed, not fewer—incorrect and ridiculous, the NRA has still blocked meaningful reforms.

## Federal, State, and Local Gun Laws

In 1981, President Reagan was ambushed outside the Washington Hilton Hotel by a 25-year-old shooter armed with a .22 caliber revolver. One bullet hit the president's chest, though he was able to joke with his surgeons, before his operation, "Please tell me you're Republicans." He also told his wife, Nancy, "Honey, I forgot to duck."[31] Reagan's press secretary, James Brady, was shot in the head and suffered partial paralysis for the rest of his life. Police officer Thomas Delahanty and Secret Service Timothy McCarthy were also shot, but both recovered. The shooter was sent to a psychiatric hospital, where he remained until his release in 2016.[32]

After the shooting, James Brady and his wife, Sarah, became advocates for gun control. Many years of advocacy led to the passage of Brady Handgun Violence Prevention Act in 1993. Often called the Brady Bill for short, the law requires background checks to be performed when a handgun is purchased from a licensed dealer. Initially, the law required a 5-day waiting period because the technology did not yet exist for instant background checks. However, the introduction of the NICS system in 1998 obviated the need for a waiting period.[33] Not since the Gun Control Act of 1968, had such significant legislation been passed. Despite its significance, the bill that was passed and signed into law, had been significantly altered and watered down due to the efforts of the NRA and sympathetic members of Congress. One such loophole is commonly called "the gun show loophole" because the law does not require background checks for guns purchased from private sellers, often at gun shows. Tragically, it is this loophole that was exploited by the two students who murdered 10 of their classmates, a teacher, and wounded 21 others at Columbine High School in 1999.[34] As of this writing, gun control advocates have not been able to get a federal law that closes the loophole and mandates universal background checks. Although there is overwhelming public support for such legislation, no bill has been passed into law at the federal level.[35] Closing this loophole should be a priority. One study found, "Nearly all (96.1%) offenders who were legally prohibited, acquired their gun from a supplier not required to conduct a background check."[36] States have taken action on their own, with 22 states and D.C. adopting laws to require a background check for some or all sales. This is a far cry from universal background checks nationwide and passing such legislation remains an important goal for gun control advocates.[37] The House of Representatives, under the speakership of Nancy Pelosi, did pass the Bipartisan Background Checks Act of 2019, but it was not taken up by the Republican-controlled Senate.

Another important issue is that of assault weapons. These weapons were banned in 1994 with the passage of the Violent Crime Control and Law Enforcement Act of 1994, but with a sunset clause that allowed the law to expire in 2004, when the ban was not renewed. Currently, seven states, plus the District of Columbia have banned assault weapons. On the campaign trail in 2020, Democratic nominee Vice President Joe Biden strongly supported an assault weapons ban, "Assault weapons—military-style firearms designed to fire rapidly—are a threat to our national security, and we should treat them as such. Anyone who pretends there's nothing we can do is lying—and holding that view should be disqualifying for anyone seeking to lead our country."[38] In contrast to the gridlock in the United States, both New Zealand and Canada banned assault weapons after mass shootings, and they did so with alacrity. New Zealand took just weeks to ban assault weapons after a white supremacist attacked two separate mosques, killing 51 worshippers and wounded 49 others.[39] Similarly, two weeks after a mass shooting in Nova Scotia, Canadian Prime Minister Justin Trudeau banned 1500 types of assault weapons.[40] Assault weapons represent a serious threat to the public safety. In the past 10 years, the seven deadliest mass shootings in the United States all involved assault weapons.[41] Moreover, such weapons account for 85.6% of deaths in mass shootings.[42] Nevertheless, the NRA has promoted assault weapons. "The AR-15 is the modern day musket," the NRA tweeted. "An everyday gun for everyday citizens."[43]

## Extreme Risk Protection Orders

Some 19 states and the District of Columbia have begun to pass extreme risk protection orders (ERPOs), often called red flag laws, that allow friends, family, and law enforcement to petition the courts to temporarily take guns away from an individuals who are showing signs of harming themselves or others.[44] The FBI found that prior to attacks, mass shooters often show signs, visible to family and friends, and with the help of ERPOs, there is a chance to prevent shootings.[45] California passed the first such law in 2016, where it is known as a gun violence restraining order (GRVO). The law has been used by law enforcement to remove weapons from 21 individuals who had threatened mass shootings in workplaces and schools. For example:

> A 21-year-old male posted a series of threatening statements on Instagram that were directed at his former high school, including, "Rip [name deleted] high school," "Nobody w[ill] be graduating from [ZIP code deleted]," "I hate all of u," "Hope I die tonight somehow," and "Dead or in jail." An acquaintance who saw the posts flagged down a police officer, and a different acquaintance reported a post that appeared to show the man holding an AR-type rifle. Both reporting parties were aware of prior school shootings and were concerned about a recurrence. The school district learned of the threats the following day and closed the school, and the subject was arrested that afternoon on a charge of making a threat with intent to terrorize. A temporary GVRO was obtained, and a 1-year order after hearing was subsequently issued.[46]

As we have seen, some states have passed laws to protect their residents from gun violence, but the nationwide laws are mired in legislative gridlock, and blocked by legislators who wish to curry favor with the NRA. Gun violence in America takes, on average, 36,000 lives every year.[47] The majority of Americans want to see gun control measures enacted. For example, 60% of Americans favor stricter laws, and 71% of Americans favor banning high capacity ammunition magazines. Some 93% of Democrats and 82% of Republicans favor closing the gun show loophole.[48]

Since government is unable to pass strong gun control measures to protect Americans, many have begun to advocate for ways to mitigate the damage and reduce deaths when mass shootings do occur.

## Stop the Bleed and Active Shooter Training

Following the tragedy of Sandy Hook Elementary School, the American Academy of Surgeons formed a committee bringing together both government and medical experts to study how to improve the chances of surviving a mass shooting by educating the public and making supplies readily available to treat devastating gun shot wounds. What emerged was a series of reports, collectively known as the Hartford Consensus, and a public education campaign known as "Stop the Bleed."[49] According to Alexander Eastman, MD, MPH, FACS, Chief of Trauma at UT Southwestern/Parkland Memorial Hospital, and Dallas Police Department Lieutenant:

> The key to improving survival in active shooter mass causality incidents is expanding the pool of first responders ... Controlling

hemorrhage has to be a core law enforcement tactic; this idea is not novel. Many lives were saved in the Tucson, AZ shooting because law enforcement responded and implemented the same techniques the Hartford Consensus is recommending. If you give these officers training and equipment to control bleeding, they will use it; they will use it well, and they will save lives.[50]

Saugus High School relied on active shooter training and used two "Stop the Bleed" kits on November 14, 2019, when a student opened fire at Saugus High School in Santa Clarita, California.[51] Two students were killed and three were injured before the gunman took his own life. The bleeding control kits had been supplied to the school by two students and their physician father, who had raised money to make the kits available

*Table 3.2* A table depicting familiarity with "Stop the Bleed" campaign and active shooter training by demographic characteristics

| % of Group | Familiarity with "Stop the Bleed" | Active shooter training |
|---|---|---|
| Male | 30.1% | 24.2% |
| Female | 26.0% | 19.0% |
| White, Non-Hispanic | 25.7% | 17.3% |
| Black, Non-Hispanic | 34.4% | 33.6% |
| White Hispanic | 32.0% | 33.3% |
| Black Hispanic | 33.3% | 33.3% |
| Unspecified Hispanic | 18.6% | 25.9% |
| Asian/Chinese/Japanese | 45.9% | 10.5% |
| Native American/American Indian/Alaska Native | 21.4% | 20.0% |
| Native Hawaiian and other Pacific Islander | 25.0% | 0.0% |
| Other Race | 100.0% | 0.0% |
| Mixed | 41.7% | 30.6% |
| Less than high school | 71.4% | 0.0% |
| High school incomplete | 33.8% | 9.2% |
| High school graduate | 24.8% | 12.9% |
| Some college, no degree | 29.4% | 26.2% |
| Two year associate's degree | 36.7% | 26.4% |
| Bachelor's degree | 27.9% | 26.8% |
| Master's degree | 32.8% | 26.6% |
| Professional or Doctorate degree | 21.4% | 31.4% |
| Under $20,000 | 31.0% | 21.3% |
| $20,000 to under $30,000 | 33.1% | 9.4% |
| $30,000 to under $40,000 | 30.0% | 16.4% |
| $40,000 to $50,000 | 31.0% | 18.1% |
| $50,000 to under $60,000 | 19.6% | 20.6% |

(*Continued*)

*Table 3.2* (Continued)

| % of Group | Familiarity with "Stop the Bleed" | Active shooter training |
|---|---|---|
| $60,000 to under $70,000 | 19.0% | 44.3% |
| $70,000 to under $100,000 | 33.9% | 21.8% |
| $100,000 to under $150,000 | 17.9% | 34.3% |
| $150,000 or more | 28.6% | 24.2% |
| 18-29 | 29.0% | 29.0% |
| 30-49 | 26.7% | 29.3% |
| 50-64 | 27.9% | 18.7% |
| 65+ | 25.7% | 4.9% |
| Non-Metro | 37.3% | 17.2% |
| Metro | 25.8% | 23.0% |
| Northeast | 26.1% | 18.0% |
| Midwest | 25.0% | 18.6% |
| South | 28.0% | 22.7% |
| West | 32.3% | 25.9% |
| Strong Republican | 38.0% | 16.5% |
| Moderate Republican | 30.6% | 23.3% |
| Leaning Republican | 30.3% | 20.0% |
| Independent | 28.1% | 20.5% |
| Leaning Democrat | 18.9% | 31.3% |
| Moderate Democrat | 24.2% | 23.5% |
| Strong Democrat | 28.9% | 16.9% |
| Extremely Conservative | 41.0% | 18.0% |
| Conservative | 32.9% | 20.0% |
| Leaning Conservative | 24.2% | 28.7% |
| Moderate | 29.1% | 16.7% |
| Leaning Liberal | 25.0% | 30.1% |
| Liberal | 18.6% | 22.7% |
| Extremely Liberal | 29.7% | 22.7% |

Source: Chapman Survey of American Fears, Wave 5, 2018. N = 1190.

district-wide. They had hoped never to use them. The availability of the kits and the quick first aid administered by a choir teacher are credited with saving lives.[52] According to the CSAF, 30.1% of men and 26% of women are familiar with "Stop the Bleed" training, see Table 3.2.

Whereas the "Stop the Bleed" campaign addresses the aftermath of a mass casualty incident, the goal of active shooter training is to prepare workplaces, houses of worship, schools, and the general public for what they should do if they find themselves confronted by a shooter. Training materials and programs are provided by law enforcement agencies, federal agencies, and private security consultants. Most teach some variation of, "Run. Hide.

Fight."[53] The training urges running from the scene as the best option. If that is not possible, then people are urged to hide from the shooter, such as in a locked office, with the lights out and the door barricaded. Finally, if one comes face to face with the shooter, it is advised to fight with anything one has available. The most popular training video was produced by Ready Houston, with expertise in emergency management and law enforcement. It shows office workers improvising weapons from a chair and a fire extinguisher and advises, "Attempt to incapacitate the shooter. Act with physical aggression. Improvise weapons. Commit to your actions."[54]

We can see in data from the CSAF that there are disparities in who receives "Stop the Bleed" and active shooter training (see Table 3.2). Men are more likely to be familiar with active shooter (24.2%) training than women (19%). Familiarity with the "Stop the Bleed" initiative and the "Run, Hide, Fight" slogan does not reduce fear of being the victim of a mass or random shooting. Similarly, having taken active shooter training at school or work does not diminish one's fear of mass shootings, according to findings in the CSAF. Only 14% of those who have had active shooter training say it reduced their fears, with 16% saying it made them more fearful, and 55.5% saying it did not impact their fear of an active shooter either way.

## Active Shooter Training in Schools and Universities

Nine out of ten public schools now drill students and faculty on what to do during a mass shooting.[55] Since 2004, the number of schools conducting active shooter drills has risen from 46.5% to 70.3% in 2014 then to 94.6% in 2016.[56] These are often traditional lockdown drills. Increasingly, these lockdown exercises are supplemented with options-based (Run, Hide, Fight or similar) drills depending on where students are developmentally and the school's action plan. Universities and colleges also routinely offer active shooter training to faculty, staff, and students.

There is currently no mandate that requires active shooter training for staff or students. Over time, these drills are changing shape and some are broadening the focus from locking doors and hiding. Options-based lockdown drills are being implemented more to give options and practice making quick decisions in intense situations. They emphasize the ability to fight back as a group, in an attempt to subdue the shooter, and suggest throwing laptops or books, rushing the shooter and doing anything to disrupt their ability to use their weapons. At Oakland University, Police Chief Mark Gordon led an active shooter training session in which the idea to throw hockey pucks at a shooter became a reality. He said, "It was just kind of a spur-of-the-moment idea that seemed to have some merit to it and it kind of caught on." As a youth hockey coach, he said the idea came from a time he was hit in the head with a puck. Tom Discenna, president of the faculty union, made a move to purchase 2500 hockey pucks monogrammed with a number that can be used to donate on the school's website.[57]

At the University of California, Berkeley, police Sergeant Sabrina Reich and Corporal Wade MacAdam ran a successful options-based drill that demonstrated the power everyone has to stop a shooter if they fight back as a group. In this drill, they first simulated a shooter entering the room where students were hiding. Not surprisingly, most of the participants were "shot." Next, the participants threw pretend laptops, books, chairs, and anything they could get their hands on at the shooter, which resulted in several shots being fired, but the assailant was subdued. Reich told students during the active shooter training, "We're not trying scare you, we don't want you to be paranoid. But we want you to be prepared."[58]

Although school shootings make up 1% of gun deaths in the country, it ranks as the second most common worry of youth aged 6–17. Some 57% of teens, aged 13–17, identified themselves as being "somewhat" or "very worried" about the possibility of a school shooting. Female, low-income, and minority students display a higher rate of worry.[59] When evaluating what kind of drills to apply to schools, it is important to keep in mind the mental development of students in addition to considering other important factors like students with special needs and prior traumatic experiences.[60] This is especially true when applying options based drills that might go beyond traditional lockdowns. As we have seen, options-based drills are often a loose adaptation of the Run, Hide, Fight that was developed for workplace violence and advocated by Homeland Security—not originally designed with students in mind.[61,62,63]

Best practices dictate that at every stage of a school drill, mental health professionals employed by the school should be prepared to address any concerns or issues that students may have.[64] The goal is to carefully monitor student reactions to drills and be available for discussion before, during, and immediately after the drill. All students and faculty should be informed of the use of props beforehand and should be able to opt out of drills, especially those that introduce airsoft guns, replica items, and other sensory elements that increase the realism of the drill. Staff should have the same option but should be required to receive comparable training.[65] For example, the staff member should be responsible for reviewing the action plan with a model of the school used to demonstrate what to do in case of a shooter. Lockdown drills should be an essential part of any emergency plan and participants should not be able to opt out as skills and preparedness gained during these drills are irreplaceable. However, options-based lockdown drills provide alternatives to traditional lockdown drills and allow students and staff to make independent decisions based on the scenario.[66]

## Activism by Survivors and Victims' Families

On Valentine's Day, 2018, a former student opened fire at Marjory Stoneman Douglas High School in Parkland, Florida, killing 17 and wounding 17 others. It is the single deadliest school shooting in the United States. The grieving Parkland community organized for gun control, with students leading the way. One student who survived the shooting, Emma Gonzalez, gave a powerful speech, just days after the shooting, at a gun control rally:

> Every single person up here today, all these people should be home grieving. But instead we are up here standing together because if all our government and President can do is send thoughts and prayers, then it's time for victims to be the change that we need to see. Since the time of the Founding Fathers and since they added the Second Amendment to the Constitution, our guns have developed at a rate that leaves me dizzy. The guns have changed but our laws have not.

We certainly do not understand why it should be harder to make plans with friends on weekends than to buy an automatic or semi-automatic weapon. In Florida, to buy a gun you do not need a permit, you do not need a gun license, and once you buy it you do not need to register it. You do not need a permit to carry a concealed rifle or shotgun. You can buy as many guns as you want at one time … If the President wants to come up to me and tell me to my face that it was a terrible tragedy and how it should never have happened and maintain telling us how nothing is going to be done about it, I'm going to happily ask him how much money he received from the National Rifle Association.
    You want to know something? It doesn't matter, because I already know. Thirty million dollars. And divided by the number of gunshot victims in the United States in the 1.5 months in 2018 alone, that comes out to being $5,800. Is that how much these people are worth to you, Trump? If you don't do anything to prevent this from continuing to occur, that number of gunshot victims will go up and the number that they are worth will go down. And we will be worthless to you. To every politician who is taking donations from the NRA, shame on you.[67]

Students have created advocacy groups and continue to push lawmakers toward gun control while encouraging voter turnout among youths. March For Our Lives and Never Again MSD are two student led groups that sprung from this tragedy. These groups advocate for several specific policies such as:[68]

- Banning semi-automatic weapons that fire high-velocity rounds
- Banning accessories that simulate automatic weapons
- Establishing a database of gun sales and universal background checks
- Changing privacy laws to allow mental healthcare providers to communicate with law enforcement
- Closing gun show and secondhand sales loopholes
- Allowing the CDC to make recommendations for gun reform
- Raising the firearm purchase age to 21
- Dedicating more funds to mental health research and professionals
- Increasing funding for school security

Outside of policy changes, the Parkland activists remind individuals not to become desensitized to gun violence and if you see something suspicious, you should say something. This reinforces the message of "See Something, Say Something®," which is a national campaign focusing on civic engagement and good faith reporting of suspicious activity (see Chapter 1). Similarly, Sandy Hook Promise, an organization founded after the shooting at Sandy Hook Elementary School in 2012, advocates a modified "See Something, Say Something®" approach called Know The Signs that attempts to teach students and faculty what to look for so that they can intervene before a perpetrator is able to carry out their plan.[69] They released a video in 2018[70] promoting Know The Signs in which students use back to school items such as socks to apply a makeshift tourniquet on a bleeding peer's leg, hold doors closed by tying them closed with a jacket and breaking windows with a skateboard to escape while gunfire is heard in the background; the video culminates in a student crouching on top of a toilet, texting her mother that she loves her as the sound of slow approaching footsteps echo in the bathroom. It's a chilling video and is not the first graphic piece of marketing material the foundation has put out but is the first to feature gunshots and blood. However, the purpose of the video is clear: disarm the violent and arm the public with knowledge of the signs to watch for.[71]

Signs to watch for are an unhealthy fascination with weapons, social withdrawal or consistent isolation, feelings of persecution, threats of violence, and antisocial behavior or if the student is marginalized socially and becomes isolated. Awareness of these warning signs can increase the chance of a student reporting unhealthy behavior that might be overlooked as a student that is simply not popular or is quiet. The program also offers training under an hour in length that is structured to be presented in a classroom or at an assembly. These programs are all provided at no cost and are in line with competencies for social-emotional learning as defined by CASEL, the Collaborative for Academic, Social, and Emotional Learning.[72]

## Guns on Campus—On Purpose?

Even as the Parkland shooting galvanized the gun control movement and schools, colleges, and universities practice drills and first aid techniques to make campuses safer, advocates for gun rights proposed a very different alternative. The National Rifle Association had proposed arming school employees, but this remained a fringe idea.[73] Following the tragedy in Parkland, the idea was thrust upon the mainstream by President Trump. "One possible solution, which may not be very popular, would be to have people in the school, teachers, administrators who have volunteered to have a firearm safely locked in the classroom," Trump said in his response to the shooting. He pitched additional ideas over the following weeks, including concealed weapons for teachers and cafeteria workers, and having undercover policemen pose as custodians. "Gun-free zone to a maniac—because they're all cowards—a gun-free zone is 'let's go in and let's attack because bullets aren't coming back at us.'"[74]

The proposal raises serious questions about the use of deadly force by school personnel. The courts have traditionally been deferential to law enforcement when they use deadly force. Often, police are given the benefit of the doubt when they use force under the standard that it seemed "objectively reasonable" in the moment. The Fourth Amendment to the Constitution prohibits unreasonable search and seizure, which includes arrest and using deadly force to take a life. That same deference has been given to school officials in court cases regarding drug testing and searches of lockers and backpacks. As government employees, teachers would face similar questions if they use deadly force in response to a perceived threat.

Moreover, there is anecdotal evidence that arming teachers and professors will lead to more shootings. For example, in Seaside, CA, a teacher demonstrating gun "safety" injured a student when his gun went off and a bullet fragment lodged in a student's neck. The wound was not life threatening and the student went home that day. His father told reporters, "I was kinda leaning toward having armed people in school in case something happened. After today, I get why people say there should be no guns in schools ... If there's an accident—people could die. If it's just one, that's more than enough."[75]

Similarly, during a chemistry class, an assistant professor at Idaho State University accidently discharged a semi-automatic weapon, shooting himself in the foot. Fortunately, there were no other injuries and the professor recovered. The incident happened after the Republican-controlled Idaho legislature passed NRA-backed legislation allowing retired law enforcement officers and individuals with concealed carry permits to bring weapons onto public college and university campuses. The law had been opposed by the colleges and universities themselves.

When we asked Americans to reflect on the safety of their neighborhood schools, compared to 20 years ago, some 89% of respondents disagreed or strongly disagreed that schools were safer and 86% correctly observed that school shootings were more prevalent. Despite this gloominess, we see reason for optimism. The public has grown weary of the NRA's arguments, with the group hitting new lows in public approval, with 48% holding favorable and 49% holding unfavorable views. This is the lowest point recorded by Gallup since 1995, when the NRA was widely criticized for trying to raise funds after the assault weapons ban.[76] Led by the powerful voices of survivors and the families of gun violence victims, we believe that the United States is at a tipping point and that meaningful reforms will be enacted at both the state and federal levels.

## Notes

1 Gun Violence Archive 2020. Mass shootings are defined as an incident when four our more people are shot, not including the shooter.
2 Martinez 2020.
3 McCullough 2019.
4 Center for Homeland Defense and Security 2020.
5 U.S. Department of Justice 2020.
6 The Guardian Staff 2020.
7 Rosen 2020.
8 Ibid.
9 Studdert et al. 2017.
10 Liu and Wiebe 2019.
11 Romer and Jamieson 2014.
12 Smith 2002.
13 Beckett 2020.
14 Barton et al. 2020.
15 Fagone et al. 2020.
16 Ibid.
17 Barton et al. 2020
18 Krebs 2020.
19 Staff, Office of U.S. Congressman Jamie Raskin 2020.

20 Collins and Zadrozny 2020.
21 Swan 2020.
22 Schleimer et al. 2020.
23 Depetris-Chauvin 2015.
24 Merod 2016.
25 The Guardian Staff 2012.
26 Ibid.
27 Keneally 2018.
28 Branas el al. 2009.
29 Moyer 2017.
30 Donohue, Aneja, and Weber 2018.
31 Rothman 2015.
32 Glass 2017.
33 Bureau of Alcohol, Tobacco, Firearms and Explosives 2019.
34 Ollinger 2015.
35 Gramlich and Schaeffer 2019.
36 Vittes et al. 2013.
37 Giffords Law Center 2020 (a).
38 Biden 2019.
39 Lopez 2019.
40 Fox 2020.
41 Giffords Law Center 2020 (b).
42 DiMaggio et al. 2019
43 NRA 2020.
44 Some gun control groups warn that the term "red flag" stigmatizes those with mental health issues and may actually assist the NRA and its allies in changing the topic from gun control to a focus on mental illness. For example, see: Coalition to Stop Gun Violence 2019.
45 Silver et al. 2018.
46 Wintemute et al. 2019.
47 Giffords Law Center 2020 (c).
48 Schaeffer 2019.
49 American College of Surgeons 2020.
50 American College of Surgeons 2013.
51 West and Kaiser Health News 2019.
52 JEMS Staff 2019.
53 Ready 2020.
54 Ready Houston 2020.
55 Campbell 2018.
56 Ibid.
57 Zaniewski 2018.
58 Fagan 2018.
59 Graf 2018.
60 National Organization for School Psychologists and National Association of School Resource Officers 2017.
61 Ready.gov 2020.
62 Carter and Sawinski 2019.
63 National School Safety and Security Services 2020.

64 National Association of School Psychologists and National Association of School Resource Officers 2017.
65 Ibid.
66 Ibid.
67 CNN Staff 2018.
68 Editorial staff of the Eagle Eye 2018.
69 Sandy Hook Promise 2016.
70 Sandy Hook Promise 2018.
71 Sanchez 2019.
72 Sandy Hook Promise 2020.
73 Abramson 2018.
74 Smith 2018.
75 Chavez and Mossburg 2018.
76 Jones 2019.

# Bibliography

Abramson, Alana. *"NRA's Wayne La Pierre: Gun Control Advocates Are Exploiting the Florida School Shooting Tragedy."* Time, February 22, 2018. https://time.com/5169511/nra-wayne-lapierre-cpac-speech/. Accessed July 28, 2020.

American College of Surgeons. *"The Hartford Consensus."* 2020. https://www.facs.org/about-acs/hartford-consensus. Accessed July 28, 2020.

American College of Surgeons. *"Stop the Bleeding! Hartford Consensus Group Issues a Call to Action."* October 9, 2013. https://www.facs.org/media/press-releases/2013/hartford1013. Accessed July 28, 2020.

Andrew Glass. *"President Reagan Shot, March 30, 1981."* POLITICO, March 3, 2017. https://www.politico.com/story/2017/03/president-reagan-shot-march-30-1981-236656. Accessed July 28, 2020.

Barton, Champe, Daniel Nass, The Trace, and Kevin Johnson. *"Gun Shops Flouted State Closure Orders in April as Industry Notched Another Big Month."* USA Today, May 15, 2020. https://www.usatoday.com/story/news/investigations/2020/05/14/gun-shops-flouted-state-coronavirus-closures-fueling-sales-boom/3115968001/. Accessed July 28, 2020.

Beckett, Lois. *"Americans Purchasing Record-Breaking Numbers of Guns amid Coronavirus."* The Guardian, April 1, 2020. http://www.theguardian.com/world/2020/apr/01/us-gun-purchases-coronavirus-record. Accessed July 28, 2020.

Biden, Joe. *"Joe Biden: Banning Assault Weapons Works."* New York Times, August 11, 2019. https://www.nytimes.com/2019/08/11/opinion/joe-biden-ban-assault-weapons.html. Accessed July 28, 2020.

Branas, Charles C., Therese S. Richmond, Dennis P. Culhane, Thomas R. Ten Have, and Douglas J. Wiebe. "Investigating the Link between Gun Possession and Gun Assault." *American Journal of Public Health 99*, no. 11 (November 1, 2009): 2034–2040. https://doi.org/10.2105/AJPH.2008.143099.

Bureau of Alcohol, Tobacco, Firearms and Explosives. *"Brady Law."* July 2, 2019. https://www.atf.gov/rules-and-regulations/brady-law. Accessed July 28, 2020.

Campbell, Alexia Fernández. *"After Parkland, a Push for More School Shooting Drills."*

*Vox*, February 16, 2018. https://www.vox.com/policy-and-politics/2018/2/16/17016382/school-shooting-drills-training. Accessed July 28, 2020.

Carter, Ken, and Beth Sawinski. "*Run-Hide-Fight or ALICE: Is It Enough to Keep Employees Safe?*" *Integrity Security Consulting and Investigations*, July 1, 2019. https://www.integritysci.com/run-hide-fight-or-alice-is-it-enough-to-keep-employees-safe/. Accessed July 28, 2020.

Center for Homeland Defense and Security. "*Mass Shooting Archives.*" *Homeland Security Digital Library*, 2020. https://www.hsdl.org/c/category/mass-shooting/. Accessed July 28, 2020.

Chavez, Nicole, and Cheri Mossburg. "*Teacher Accidentally Fires Gun and Injures Student in California.*" *CNN*, March 15, 2018. https://www.cnn.com/2018/03/14/us/california-teacher-fires-gun/index.html. Accessed July 28, 2020.

CNN Staff. "*Florida Student Emma Gonzalez to Lawmakers and Gun Advocates: 'We Call BS.'*" *CNN*, February 17, 2018. https://www.cnn.com/2018/02/17/us/florida-student-emma-gonzalez-speech/index.html. Accessed July 28, 2020.

Coalition to Stop Gun Violence. "*It's Time to Retire the Term 'Red Flag Laws.'*" *Giffords Law Center*, March 26, 2019. https://giffords.org/blog/2019/03/retire-red-flag-laws/. Accessed July 28, 2020.

Collins, Ben, and Brandy Zadrozny. "*In Trump's 'LIBERATE' Tweets, Extremists See a Call to Arms.*" *NBC News*, April 17, 2020. https://www.nbcnews.com/tech/security/trump-s-liberate-tweets-extremists-see-call-arms-n1186561. Accessed July 28, 2020.

Depetris-Chauvin, Emilio. "Fear of Obama: An Empirical Study of the Demand for Guns and the U.S. 2008 Presidential Election." *Journal of Public Economic 130* (October 1, 2015): 66–79. https://doi.org/10.1016/j.jpubeco.2015.04.008.

DiMaggio, Charles, Jacob Avraham, Cherisse Berry, Marko Bukur, Justin Feldman, Michael Klein, Noor Shah, Manish Tandon, and Spiros Frangos. "Changes in US Mass Shooting Deaths Associated with the 1994-2004 Federal Assault Weapons Ban: Analysis of Open-Source Data." *Journal of Trauma and Acute Care Surgery 86*, no. 1 (January 2019): 11–19. https://doi.org/10.1097/TA.0000000000002060.

Donohue, John J., Abhay Aneja, and Kyle D. Weber. "*Right-To-Carry Laws and Violent Crime: A Comprehensive Assessment Using Panel Data and A State-Level Synthetic Control Analysis.*" Working Paper,. National Bureau of Economic Research, November 2018. https://www.nber.org/papers/w23510.pdf. Accessed July 28, 2020.

Editorial Staff of the Eagle Eye. "*Parkland Students: Our Manifesto to Change America's Gun Laws | Editorial Staff of the Eagle Eye.*" *The Guardian*, March 23, 2018. https://www.theguardian.com/us-news/commentisfree/2018/mar/23/parkland-students-manifesto-americas-gun-laws. Accessed July 28, 2020.

Fagan, Kevin. "*Mass Shootings Are on the Rise. So Are Classes on How to Avoid Them.*" *San Francisco Chronicle*, January 2, 2018. https://www.sfchronicle.com/bayarea/article/Mass-shootings-are-on-the-rise-So-are-classes-on-12466219.php. Accessed July 28, 2020.

Fagone, Jason, Matthias Gafni, Tatiana Sanchez, and Nanette Asimov. "*Gun Sales Surge amid Coronavirus Fears—and Lockdown.*" *San Francisco Chronicle*,

March 17, 2020. https://www.sfchronicle.com/bayarea/article/Gun-sales-surge-amid-coronavirus-fears-and-15138650.php. Accessed July 28, 2020.

Fox, James Alan. "*Canada Bans Assault Weapons after Mass Shooting. The Contrast with US Inaction Is Painful.*" *USA Today*, May 5, 2020. https://www.usatoday.com/story/opinion/2020/05/05/canada-shooting-assault-weapons-ban-trump-senate-inaction-column/3084317001/. Accessed July 28, 2020.

Giffords Law Center. "*Assault Weapons.*" Giffords Law Center to Prevent Gun Violence, 2020a. https://lawcenter.giffords.org/gun-laws/policy-areas/hardware-ammunition/assault-weapons/. Accessed July 28, 2020.

Giffords Law Center. "*Gun Violence Statistics.*" Giffords Law Center to Prevent Gun Violence, 2020b. https://lawcenter.giffords.org/facts/gun-violence-statistics/. Accessed July 28, 2020.

Giffords Law Center. "*Universal Background Checks.*" Giffords Law Center to Prevent Gun Violence, 2020c. https://lawcenter.giffords.org/gun-laws/policy-areas/background-checks/universal-background-checks/. Accessed July 28, 2020.

Graf, Nikki. "*Majority of Teens Worry about School Shootings, and Most Parents Share Their Concern.*" *Pew Research Center*, April 18, 2018. https://www.pewresearch.org/fact-tank/2018/04/18/a-majority-of-u-s-teens-fear-a-shooting-could-happen-at-their-school-and-most-parents-share-their-concern/. Accessed July 28, 2020.

Gramlich, John, and Katherine Schaeffer. "*7 Facts about Guns in the U.S.*" *Pew Research Center*, October 22, 2019. https://www.pewresearch.org/fact-tank/2019/10/22/facts-about-guns-in-united-states/. Accessed July 28, 2020.

Gun Violence Archive. "Past Summary Ledgers." 2020. https://www.gunviolencearchive.org/past-tolls. Accessed July 28, 2020.

JEMS Staff. "*Stop the Bleed Training and Kits Prove Their Worth at Calif. School Shooting.*" *Journal of Emergency Medical Services*, November 15, 2019. https://www.jems.com/2019/11/15/stop-the-bleed-training-and-kits-prove-their-worth-at-calif-school-shooting/. Accessed July 28, 2020.

Jones, Jeffrey M. "*Americans' Views of NRA Become Less Positive.*" *Gallup*, September 13, 2019. https://news.gallup.com/poll/266804/americans-views-nra-become-less-positive.aspx. Accessed July 28, 2020.

Keneally, Meghan. "*Breaking down the NRA-Backed Theory That a Good Guy with a Gun Stops a Bad Guy with a Gun.*" *ABC News*, October 29, 2018. https://abcnews.go.com/US/breaking-nra-backed-theory-good-guy-gun-stops/story?id=53360480. Accessed July 28, 2020.

Krebs, Christopher C. "*Advisory Memorandum on Identification of Essential Critical Infrastructure Workers During COVID-19 Response.*" U.S. Department of Homeland Security, March 28, 2020. https://www.cisa.gov/sites/default/files/publications/Version_3.0_CISA_Guidance_on_Essential_Critical_Infrastructure_Workers_1.pdf. Accessed July 28, 2020.

Liu, Gina, and Douglas J. Wiebe. "A Time-Series Analysis of Firearm Purchasing After Mass Shooting Events in the United States." *JAMA Network Open 2*, no. 4 (April 5, 2019): e191736. https://doi.org/10.1001/jamanetworkopen.2019.1736.

Lopez, German. "*New Zealand Parliament Votes 119-1 to Ban Assault Weapons, Less than *a Month after a Mass Shooting." Vox*, April 10, 2019. https://www.vox.com/2019/4/10/18304415/new-zealand-gun-control-mosque-shootings-assault-weapons-ban. Accessed July 28, 2020.

Martinez, Peter. *"El Paso Mass Shooting Survivor Celebrates First Birthday without His Parents." CBS News*, May 25, 2020. https://www.cbsnews.com/news/el-paso-mass-shooting-survivor-celebrates-first-birthday-2020-05-25/. Accessed July 28, 2020.

McCullough, Jolie. *"El Paso Shooting Suspect Said He Ordered His AK-47 and Ammo from Overseas." Texas Tribune*, August 28, 2019. https://www.texastribune.org/2019/08/28/el-paso-shooting-gun-romania/. Accessed July 28, 2020.

Merod, Anna. *"How the NRA Has Responded to Mass Shootings over the Years." NBC News*, June 15, 2016. https://www.nbcnews.com/storyline/orlando-nightclub-massacre/how-nra-has-responded-mass-shootings-over-years-n592551. Accessed July 28, 2020.

Moyer, Melinda Wenner. "More Guns Do Not Stop More Crimes, Evidence Shows." *Scientific American*, October 1, 2017. https://doi.org/10.1038/scientificamerican1017-54.

National Association of School Psychologists, and National Association of School Resource Officers. *"Best Practice Considerations for Schools in Active Shooter and Other Armed Assailant Drills."* National Association of School Psychologists, April 2017. https://www.nasponline.org/resources-and-publications/resources-and-podcasts/school-climate-safety-and-crisis/systems-level-prevention/best-practice-considerations-for-schools-in-active-shooter-and-other-armed-assailant-drills. Accessed July 28, 2020.

National School Safety and Security Services. *"ALICE & Run-Hide-Fight Training: Teaching Students to Attack Gunmen."* 2020. https://www.schoolsecurity.org/trends/alice-training/. Accessed July 28, 2020.

NRA. *"The AR-15 is the modern day musket. An everyday gun for everyday citizens."* Twitter, July 11, 2020. https://twitter.com/NRA/status/1282041621169819648. Accessed July 28, 2020.

Ollinger, David. *"Massacre Energizes Gun Debate – but Not Lawmakers." Denver Post*, April 19, 2015. https://extras.denverpost.com/news/col0419g.htm. Accessed July 28, 2020.

Ready. *"Active Shooter." Ready.gov*, April 22, 2020. https://www.ready.gov/active-shooter. Accessed July 28, 2020.

Ready Houston. *"RUN. HIDE. FIGHT.® Surviving an Active Shooter Event."* YouTube, 2012. Accessed July 28, 2020. https://www.youtube.com/watch?v=5VcSwejU2D0.

Romer, Daniel, and Patrick Jamieson. "Violence in Popular U.S. Prime Time TV Dramas and the Cultivation of Fear: A Time Series Analysis." *Media and Communication 2*, no. 2 (June 17, 2014): 31–41. https://doi.org/10.17645/mac.v2i2.8.

Rosen, Jeffrey F. *"Report on the Non-Fatal Shooting of Santino Legan."* Santa Clara County: District Attorney, March 10, 2020. https://htv-prod-media.s3.amazonaws.com/files/gilroy-garlic-festival-shooting-report-1583860207.pdf. Accessed July 28, 2020.

Rothman, Lily. "*Read President Reagan's Best Jokes about Being Shot.*" *Time*, March 30, 2015. https://time.com/3752477/reagan-assassination-reaction/. Accessed July 28, 2020.

Sanchez, Olivia. "*Latest Sandy Hook Promise PSA Gives Nightmarish Look at School Shootings.*" *USA Today*, September 18, 2019. https://www.usatoday.com/story/news/nation/2019/09/18/sandy-hook-promise-psa-gives-graphic-look-school-shootings/2301317001/. Accessed July 28, 2020.

Sandy Hook Promise. "*Do You Know the Signs?*" YouTube, 2018. Accessed July 28, 2020. https://www.youtube.com/watch?v=FT7Q_Gn8eIk.

Sandy Hook Promise. "*Know the Signs.*" Sandy Hook Promise, 2016. https://nationalsave.org/wp-content/uploads/2018/01/SHP_Know_the_Signs_Guide.pdf. Accessed July 28, 2020.

Sandy Hook Promise. "*Know the Signs Programs.*" 2020. https://www.sandyhookpromise.org/prevention-programs2. Accessed July 28, 2020.

Schaeffer, Katherine. "*Share of Americans Who Favor Stricter Gun Laws Has Increased since 2017.*" *Pew Research Center*, October 16, 2019. https://www.pewresearch.org/fact-tank/2019/10/16/share-of-americans-who-favor-stricter-gun-laws-has-increased-since-2017/. Accessed July 28, 2020.

Schleimer, Julia P., Christopher D. McCort, Veronia A. Pear, Aaron Shev, Elizabeth Tomsich, Rameesha Asif-Sattar, Shani Buggs, Hannah S. Laqueur, and Garen J. Wintemute. "*Firearm Purchasing and Firearm Violence in the First Months of the Coronavirus Pandemic in the United States.*" *MedRxiv* (July 11, 2020): 1–19. https://doi.org/10.1101/2020.07.02.20145508.

Silver, James, Andre Simons, and Sarah Craun. "*A Study of the Pre-Attack Behaviors of Active Shooters in the United States between 2000 and 2013.*" Federal Bureau of Investigation, U.S. Department of Justice, June 2018. https://www.fbi.gov/file-repository/pre-attack-behaviors-of-active-shooters-in-us-2000-2013.pdf. Accessed July 28, 2020.

Smith, David. "*Trump's Solution to School Shootings: Arm Teachers with Guns.*" *The Guardian*, February 21, 2018. https://www.theguardian.com/us-news/2018/feb/21/donald-trump-solution-to-school-shootings-arm-teachers-with-guns. Accessed July 28, 2020.

Smith, Tom W. "*Surge in Gun Sales? The Press Misfires.*" *Public Perspective*, 2002, July/August. https://ropercenter.cornell.edu/sites/default/files/2018-07/134005.pdf. Accessed July 28, 2020.

Staff. "*Members of Congress Call on Homeland Security to Drop Gun Shops from Essential Business List.*" Office of U.S. Congressman Jamie Raskin, April 9, 2020. https://raskin.house.gov/media/press-releases/members-congress-call-homeland-security-drop-gun-shops-essential-business-list. Accessed July 28, 2020.

Staff. "*NRA: Full Statement by Wayne LaPierre in Response to Newtown Shootings.*" *The Guardian*, December 21, 2012. http://www.theguardian.com/world/2012/dec/21/nra-full-statement-lapierre-newtown. Accessed July 28, 2020.

Staff. "*Texas Man Accused in El Paso Mass Shooting Charged with Federal Hate Crime.*" *The Guardian*, February 6, 2020. http://www.theguardian.com/us-news/2020/feb/06/el-paso-walmart-shooting-hate-crime. Accessed July 28, 2020.

Studdert, David M., Yifan Zhang, Jonathan A. Rodden, Rob J. Hyndman, and Garen J. Wintemute. "Handgun Acquisitions in California After Two Mass Shootings." *Annals of Internal Medicine 166*, no. 10 (May 16, 2017): 698–706. https://doi.org/10.7326/M16-1574.

Swan, Betsy Woodruff. *"Trump Justice Department Asks for More Resources to Enforce Gun Laws."* *POLITICO*, May 12, 2020. https://www.politico.com/news/2020/05/12/justice-department-resources-gun-laws-252398. Accessed July 28, 2020.

U.S. Department of Justice. *"Texas Man Charged with Federal Hate Crimes and Firearm Offenses Related to August 3, 2019, Mass-Shooting in El Paso."* *U.S. Attorney's Office Western District of Texas News*, February 6, 2020. https://www.justice.gov/usao-wdtx/pr/texas-man-charged-federal-hate-crimes-and-firearm-offenses-related-august-3-2019-mass. Accessed July 28, 2020.

Vittes, Katherine A., Jon S. Vernick, and Daniel W. Webster. "Legal Status and Source of Offenders' Firearms in States with the Least Stringent Criteria for Gun Ownership." *Injury Prevention: Journal of the International Society for Child and Adolescent Injury Prevention 19*, no. 1 (February 2013): 26–31. https://doi.org/10.1136/injuryprev-2011-040290.

West, Sandy, and Kaiser Health News. *"Books, Binders and Bleed-Control Kits: How School Shootings Are Changing Classroom Basics."* *NBC News*, December 8, 2019. https://www.nbcnews.com/health/health-news/books-binders-bleed-control-kits-how-school-shootings-are-changing-n1097276. Accessed July 28, 2020.

Wintemute, Garen J., Veronica A. Pear, Julia P. Schleimer, Rocco Pallin, Sydney Sohl, Nicole Kravitz-Wirtz, and Elizabeth A. Tomsich. "Extreme Risk Protection Orders Intended to Prevent Mass Shootings." *Annals of Internal Medicine 171*, no. 9 (August 20, 2019): 655–658. https://doi.org/10.7326/M19-2162.

Zaniewski, Ann. *"Oakland University Using Hockey Pucks to Protect against Active Shooters."* *Detroit Free Press*, November 28, 2018. https://www.freep.com/story/news/local/michigan/oakland/2018/11/27/oakland-university-hockey-pucks/2129677002/. Accessed July 28, 2020.

# 4 Conspiracy Theories and Mass Shootings

Within hours of the deadliest mass shooting in modern U.S. history, misinformation and conspiracy theories began to circulate.[1] The shooting at an outdoor concert in Las Vegas, in 2017, left 58 people dead and over 800 wounded. Trolls on 4Chan misidentified the shooter and the story spread quickly after a right-wing blog, *The Gateway Pundit*, published the hoax, without regard to its veracity.[2] The story spread widely due to Facebook and Google searches.[3] Even after the identity of the shooter was well-known and the misinformation regarding who did the shooting was corrected, conspiracies picked up steam. On his *InfoWars* show, Alex Jones spewed dozens of theories about the Las Vegas shooter, his family, and his motives.[4] At one point he declared, "This is a Democratic Party production—I will say it. They did it. They've been calling for a civil war, they've been calling to kill conservatives, they want our guns, they're completely obvious, and they're just—it's incredible."[5]

The notion that a mass shooting is a staged event to encourage widespread support of gun control measures is a common theme. Sometimes, shootings are described as a "false flag" attack, where the government is believed to be responsible for carrying out the attack on its own people. Other times, the claim is that the attack never happened at all. This is where the concept of "crisis actors" becomes central to conspiracies. The presence of actors and fake blood help to explain away pictures and videos taken at the scene.

In addition to Alex Jones, YouTube was flooded with videos claiming to reveal that the dead and wounded in Las Vegas were "crisis actors" and that nobody died. Even after they were removed from YouTube, such videos remain online. For example, while rolling gory footage of the scene in Las Vegas, one conspiracy theorist tells viewers that the video confirms his contention that nobody died. His video received some 16,000 views. He tells viewers:

> Alright, welcome to another crisis actor staged event hoax. The first gentleman has his legs crossed with the red sock. Second gentleman,

we're gonna make sure everyone sees our hand here, our red, bloody hand, look at my hand, look at my hand, look at my hand. He's got blood on it... O-kay... And this'll be our first scene. And what we're gonna do is we make sure we have our script right, and we're gonna pull up and make sure that we have a little bit of our fake blood on it... is there any? Well, we forgot to put the fake blood on... Maybe he's not dead. Maybe he's breathing. Okay... um... It's going pretty well so far. And now, here we go, we're gonna walk into... some blood! Or it looks like blood... Looks like paint... Uh, someone last night says "watery, and too bright red for me." Now notice the shadow on this lady. See the shadow? That's his lanyard. That's his—that's his crisis pass. His crisis actor pass that the security guard will make sure in the end that he shows him.[6]

Because proponents of the crisis actor conspiracy contend that the mass shooting was faked with the help of actors, they often harass the victims via social media and accuse them of perpetuating the hoax.[7] Braden Matejka was shot in the head and survived. His family turned to Facebook and GoFundMe to raise money for his medical bills. Conspiracy theorists left vicious messages. A few of the messages were quoted by *The Guardian*:

"Obviously a TERRIBLE CRISIS ACTOR," wrote a Facebook user named Samantha. "HE'S SCAMMING THE PUBLIC ... This was a government set up."

"YOUR A LIAR AND THEFT PIECE OF CRAP [sic]," wrote Karen.

"You'll pay on the other side," said a user named Mach. Others called Braden a "LYING BASTARD", "scumbag govt actor" and "fuckin FRAUD", while one user named Josh wrote: "I hope someone comes after you and literally beats the living fuck outa you."

Eventually, Braden deleted his social media accounts, he told *The Guardian* newspaper.[8] Braden was just one of many survivors who were harangued and accused of faking their injuries. To this day, videos abound on the Internet. Some videos are posted to show evidence of what happened, whereas others are used to bolster the claims of conspiracy theorists that the incident never occurred. Regardless of intent, such videos often cause further trauma to victims, at the same time they lead others to question reality.[9]

The Las Vegas incident is not the only instance of a mass shooting being labeled a hoax. In fact, every mass shooting since Sandy Hook has spawned conspiracy theories and claims that the victims were actually "crisis actors." The term "crisis actors" emerged following the tragedy at Sandy Hook and appears to have been inspired by the use of actors to role-play victims in training emergency medical personnel and others for mass casualty events.[10] A series of online posts to Memory Hole Blog questioned what happened at Sandy Hook, "While it sounds like an outrageous claim, one is left to inquire whether the Sandy Hook shooting ever took place—at least in the way law enforcement authorities and the nation's news media have described."[11] Alex Jones, with a considerably bigger audience, continued promoting the idea that Sandy Hook was a hoax for years.[12] The blog is still a destination for conspiracy theorists that now has a focus on spreading a variety of conspiracy theories, including those related to COVID-19 and the Black Lives Matter movement.

The conspiracy theory was also promoted in a book entitled, "Nobody Died at Sandy Hook: It was a FEMA Drill Designed to Promote Gun Control." The book was published in 2015 and a 2nd "revised and expanded" edition was published in 2017. The authors and the publisher were sued by Sandy Hook parents. The book's publisher apologized to Lenny Pozner, the father of 6-year-old Noah who was murdered at Sandy Hook.[13] Pozner was awarded damages and told *NPR*, "I think it gives people who are also attacked and victimized online the confidence that this is something that can go to court and that you can win. It feels good to win and stand up for Noah's life—very short life."[14] Some 10 years after the tragedy, victims' families continue to be harassed by conspiracy theorists.[15] The Pozners moved seven times over the course of 5 years due to the constant harassment and even death threats.

As we saw in Chapter 2, following the tragedy at Marjory Stoneman Douglas High School, students who survived spoke out and they were attacked by right-wing media.[16] YouTube had to apologize after a video claiming the shooting was hoax began trending.[17] Eventually, it was taken down. Many more continued to spring up. One outspoken student, David Hogg, who had survived the attack, went on CNN to declare, "I'm not a crisis actor."[18] In that same interview, Anderson Cooper pointed out that conspiracy theories about Hogg were being spread by Twitter and that they had gotten a boost when the president's son, Donald Trump Jr., liked one of the tweets. Similarly, an NRA board member, Ted Nugent, liked a comment on Facebook that claimed Hogg was a crisis actor, thus helping to keep the hoax going. Nugent also called the students who survived, "mushy brained children" and "liars."[19] Numerous right-wing media personalities attempted to bully the Parkland students, but they stood firm. After Lauran Ingraham mocked David Hogg on Twitter, and he responded by noting sponsors of her show, she quickly had to apologize because her Fox news program was losing those sponsors.[20] The Parkland teens were—and are—a force to be reckoned with.

## Belief in Mass Shooting Conspiracies

Unfortunately, conspiracy theories about mass shootings are not confined to Twitter trolls and those like Alex Jones who make a living off trafficking in wild hoaxes. In fact, the CSAF found that 42.7% of Americans agree or strongly agree that the government is concealing what it knows about mass shootings, such as those at Sandy Hook, Las Vegas, and Parkland.

To examine belief in this conspiracy theory, we analyzed a variety of factors that contribute to these beliefs (see Table 4.1). We find that partisanship predicts belief, with Republicans being more likely than Democrats to buy into the idea of a conspiracy. Relying heavily on social media or FOX for news also predicts belief, as does fear of the government restricting firearms and ammunitions. Those who rely on national newspapers are less likely to think the government is hiding what it knows about Sandy Hook, Las Vegas, and Parkland. Of all these factors, the fear of government curbing ownership of guns and ammunition has the strongest relationship on belief. Moreover, some 37.9% of Americans are afraid or very afraid of such restrictions.

We also compared belief in a Sandy Hook conspiracy to belief in the South Dakota crash, a conspiracy wholly created by us to use as a kind of baseline. We have reported elsewhere that more than half of the respondents to the CSAF believed in multiple conspiracy theories, ranging from JFK (61%) to the enduring Illuminati conspiracies (43%) and some 32% agreed or strongly agreed that the government was concealing information on the South Dakota crash.[21]

Table 4.2 shows a general willingness to believe in alternative explanations and resistance to accepting information that comes from the government. Traditionally, conspiracists reject the general discourse rather than proffering their own evidence. If there is any evidence to be seen, it is often inconclusive and the argument given is one of loose connections and half facts; naturally making arguing *against* the accepted norm an easier task. Conspiracism is rooted in mistrust and operates in tandem with belief that we are being lied to in a large amount of official transmissions.[22] We can also see some variation in belief based on demographic variables. For example, residents of the Northeast are the most likely to say they believe the government is concealing what it knows about mass shootings (46.9%) than others. We can also see women are more likely than men to say they buy into both conspiracies, 38.7% vs. 25.1% and 47.6% vs. 37.2%, respectively.

Table 4.1 OLS Regression Predicting Belief in Sandy Hook/Las Vegas/Parkland Conspiracies by Media Use

| Variables | b | β |
|---|---|---|
| Ideology | .029 | .045 |
| Party | −.071** | −.115 |
| Local Newspaper | .034 | .054 |
| National Newspaper | .073** | .117 |
| Network News | −.036 | −.060 |
| Fox News | −.078** | −.131 |
| CNN | .000 | .000 |
| MSNBC | −.020 | −.030 |
| Local TV News | .033 | .055 |
| Talk Radio | .022 | .035 |
| Web | .016 | .025 |
| Social Media | −.099** | −.178 |
| Fear of Gun Control | .211** | .242 |
| **Model stats** | | |
| Constant | 2.405 | |
| N | 1190 | |
| Adjusted $R^2$ | .132 | |

Source: 2018 CSAF***$p < .001$; **$p < .01$; *$p < .05$ (two-tailed tests).

Party yielded more noticeable differences with respect to Sandy Hook/Parkland/Las Vegas, than our invented conspiracy, with Republicans and Independents more likely to agree or strongly agree that the government was withholding information. We can see some differences due to race/ethnicity as well. Again, the pattern is more pronounced for the mass shooting conspiracy than for the South Dakota crash. However, the South Dakota crash has more takers among those without a high school education. Notably, both conspiracies had a substantial number of believers at all levels of education. Some 19.2% of those with a postgraduate degree believed in an invented South Dakota crash conspiracy and 24.1% subscribe to the mass shooting conspiracies associated with Sandy Hook, Las Vegas, and Parkland. This demonstrates that education cannot be counted on to combat belief in conspiracy theories. Overall, Table 4.2 shows that belief in conspiracy theories is widespread and endemic throughout society.

## Understanding Belief in Conspiracy Theories

Motivations may be more important than demographic characteristics in understanding why so many Americans believe one or more conspiracy theories. One study found three key characteristics that predict belief:

*Table 4.2* Belief in the Sandy Hook and South Dakota Crash Conspiracies by Demographics

| % of Group | South Dakota Crash | Sandy Hook Shooting |
|---|---|---|
| Male | 25.1% | 37.2% |
| Female | 38.7% | 47.6% |
| White, Non-Hispanic | 27.6% | 39.4% |
| Black, Non-Hispanic | 53.0% | 60.6% |
| White Hispanic | 35.8% | 48.0% |
| Black Hispanic | 33.3% | 10.0% |
| Unspecified Hispanic | 24.1% | 41.4% |
| Asian/Chinese/Japanese | 29.7% | 37.8% |
| Native American/Alaska Native | 73.3% | 28.6% |
| Native Hawaiian/Pacific Islander | 0.0% | 50.0% |
| Mixed | 41.6% | 45.9% |
| Less than High School | 87.5% | 37.5% |
| High School Incomplete | 51.6% | 61.0% |
| High School Graduate | 36.3% | 51.5% |
| Some College, No Degree | 34.2% | 45.7% |
| Two-Year Associate Degree | 34.5% | 35.5% |
| Four-Year University Degree | 21.6% | 30.7% |
| Some Postgraduate Schooling | 30.2% | 43.7% |
| Postgraduate or Professional Degree | 19.2% | 24.1% |
| 18–29 | 45.5% | 54.4% |
| 30–49 | 31.6% | 46.5% |
| 50–64 | 26.8% | 39.6% |
| 65+ | 23.4% | 27.3% |
| Northeast | 35.5% | 46.9% |
| Midwest | 27.7% | 36.7% |
| South | 32.7% | 41.2% |
| West | 27.7% | 29.8% |
| Under $20,000 | 49.1% | 57.8% |
| $20,000–$29,999 | 47.4% | 58.1% |
| $30,000–$39,999 | 35.0% | 46.4% |
| $40,000–$49,999 | 29.5% | 66.7% |
| $50,000–$59,999 | 28.5% | 48.5% |
| $60,000–$69,999 | 20.5% | 24.1% |
| $70,000–$99,999 | 17.3% | 26.1% |
| $100,000–$149,999 | 23.9% | 29.6% |
| $150,000 or more | 23.1% | 31.9% |
| Center City (Metro) | 29.7% | 41.1% |
| Center City County (Metro) | 27.8% | 43.9% |
| Suburban (Metro) | 27.6% | 39.2% |
| Non-Center City (Metro) | 32.0% | 49.1% |
| Non-Metro | 40.3% | 38.2% |
| Strong Republican | 30.8% | 41.3% |
| Moderate Republican | 23.2% | 41.1% |

(*Continued*)

Table 4.2 (Continued)

| % of Group | South Dakota Crash | Sandy Hook Shooting |
|---|---|---|
| Leaning Republican | 25.2% | 38.4% |
| Independent | 38.6% | 51.9% |
| Leaning Democrat | 29.1% | 39.1% |
| Moderate Democrat | 30.2% | 32.6% |
| Strong Democrat | 30.3% | 31.7% |
| Extremely Conservative | 35.0% | 50.9% |
| Conservative | 35.3% | 49.5% |
| Leaning Conservative | 16.9% | 31.0% |
| Moderate | 42.0% | 53.0% |
| Leaning Liberal | 25.2% | 31.9% |
| Liberal | 19.3% | 27.7% |
| Extremely Liberal | 36.0% | 36.0% |

Source: Chapman Survey of American Fears, 2019.

> Belief in conspiracy theories appears to be driven by motives that can be characterized as epistemic (understanding one's environment), existential (being safe and in control of one's environment), and social (maintaining a positive image of the self and the social group).[23]

Thus, those who adhere to such beliefs receive a great deal of psychological reward. One need not process the grief and tragedy of a shooting if it never even happened. Or, if it did happen, there is an explanation that makes the event seem less random—it was planned as a "false flag" attack. Moreover, if one's political and ideological beliefs demand opposition to gun control measures, then believing that shootings are staged events with actors, for the sole purpose of swaying public opinion, allows believers to brush off calls for new laws.

Another important factor motivating belief is anomia, or disaffection with society and belief that things are getting worse.[24] One survey operationalized anomia as the belief that the average person's situation is getting worse as time goes on, that it was unfair to bring a child into the world and that the majority of public officials are not interested in the average man and have motivations that are beyond serving public interest.[25] The study found anomia was correlated with belief in conspiracy and is linked with feelings of alienation and exclusion from the system. During times of insecurity and discontent there is often a need to place blame on an external actor to channel feelings of anger and discontent. A conspiracy theory gives a psychological outlet to channel these feelings and an object on which to place blame. For many, this is less confusing than simply being angry because of a situation one has little control over.

Conspiracy theories also appear to appeal to those who feel their positive self-image or position in the in-group to be threatened. This allows for a more positive self-identification and can work as a method of deflecting negative outcomes since those outcomes can be attributed to the conspirators.[26] While conspiracy theories may fulfill psychological needs for some, the information is not accurate, and the drawbacks of conspiratorial thought are not acknowledged by believers as this shifts to be their truth. This is correlated to a lower ability or desire to think critically and analytically[27] while also showing a relation to lower levels of education.[28]

Conspiracy beliefs are adopted by those that feel anxious, powerless, or lacking in control of their surroundings. One study showed that belief in conspiracy is reduced when participants felt they had greater control and heightened when outcomes felt out of their control.[29] Exposure to conspiracy decreases trust in government, scientists, and politicians, even if the theories were independent of these organizations.[30] This forces conspiracists to the "out group" and can prevent them from seeing themselves as valuable members of mainstream society.

A common connector of conspiracists is that they suffer from a "crippled epistemology," meaning they possess little knowledge as a whole and the information they do possess is wrong in one form or another.[31] Cass Sunstein argues this is the basis for extremists who are not irrational, but act upon views that are supported by their scarce and incorrect information. This, in conjunction with resistance to contrary evidence, creates an environment of active distrust towards the actors these theories target. These theories are frequently regarding government actors who are already subjects of distrust for many who are uneducated, making it exceedingly difficult to disprove these theories as counterfactuals are taken to be inventions by the suspected shadowy forces that are driving these theories to begin with.

In line with a crippled epistemology, conspiracy theories often form monological belief systems that are entirely made up of self-confirming beliefs. Even incompatible theories show a positive correlation of endorsement as they hold the same belief that governmental agents are withholding information from the public.[32] As an example of this, the belief that Osama bin Laden is still alive shows no negative correlation to believing he has been dead for years. The belief is simply that the public is being deceived.

This is to say that belief in conspiracy theories is driven by alternatives that are not as simple as being correlated due to prior belief in these theories, rather that there are more broad beliefs or psychological needs that are driving belief.[33] Even so, belief in one theory is the best predictor of belief in any other theory as genuine belief in any theory begins to establish governmental authority as fundamentally deceptive. As this idea becomes stronger and stronger, it becomes easier for the conspiracist to disagree with the official narrative and adopt other theories due to active distrust in the authoritative body.[34] This is an important distinction to make as research previously suggested the relationship between conspiracy theories to be based only on belief in one theory but this shows that, while still monological in nature, theories do not directly support each other but instead support the idea of high order deception and conspiracy in general.[35]

Peer influence also plays a role in establishing or rejecting conspiracy belief. Despite knowing what is correct, the individual may still acquiesce to social pressure that the group creates.[36,37] Many conspiracists seek to be a part of the in group by any means necessary. This includes buying into a conspiracy theory as a way of creating perceived uniqueness in the form of possessing scarce information.[38]

Conspiratorial beliefs lead the way to both group and attitude polarization, which can eventually lead to extremism and violence, given conditions for incubation.[39] Attitude polarization is the case where those of similar ideas come to more extreme conclusions after discussion. With conspiracy beliefs, these interchanges can lead to greater adherence to alternative theories. Importantly, they can expand on fringe ideas that can ultimately lead to violence.[40] Such was the case of the pizzagate conspiracy in which believers thought children were being held in the basement of a pizza parlor called Comet Ping Pong, in connection with a child sex trafficking ring involving Hillary Clinton and other Democratic Party leaders. One man armed with an assault weapon stormed into the pizza shop and began shooting. Nobody was injured and the assailant surrendered to police after he discovered there was no basement and no children being held.[41]

## Conclusion

Conspiracy theories might seem like a new addition to America's politics, born of the Internet; however, Americans have long held a conspiratorial mind-set, as explained in Richard Hofstadter's *The Paranoid Style in American Politics*. Hofstadter uses examples such as the 18th-century panic of over the "Bavarian Illuminati" that was sparked in 1797 with the publication of *Proofs of Conspiracy Against All the Religions and Governments of Europe Carried on in the Secret Meetings of Free Masons, Illuminati, and Reading Societies*. More was written on this topic and the conspiracy picked up steam, with added layers that became fodder for pulpits across New England.[42] Hofstadter explores a variety of conspiracies from the 19th and 20th centuries and sums up the "basic elements in the paranoid style":

The central image is that of a vast and sinister commotion to undermine and destroy a way of life. One may object that there *are* conspiratorial acts in history, and there is nothing paranoid about taking note of them. This is true. All political behavior requires strategy, many strategic acts depend for the effect upon a period of secrecy, and anything that is secret may be described, often with but little exaggeration, as conspiratorial. The distinguishing thing about the paranoid style is not that its exponents see conspiracies or plots here and there in history, but that they regard a "vast" or "gigantic" conspiracy as *the motive force* in historical events. History *is* a conspiracy, set in motion by demonic forces of almost transcendent power...The paranoid spokesman sees the fate of this conspiracy in apocalyptic terms—he traffics in the birth and death of whole worlds, whole political orders, whole systems of human values. He is always manning the barricades of civilization. He constantly lives at a turning point: it is now or never in organizing resistance to conspiracy. Time is forever just running out.[43]

However, Hofstadter could never have imagined an America where the paranoia had reached the White House, with Hofstadter's "paranoid spokesman" embodied by the commander in chief, whose tweets have fueled conspiracy theories.[44] QAnon incorporates pizzagate, along with an ever-growing body of conspiracies that involve "the deep state" cover-up of a pedophile ring, cannibalism, and Satanic rituals.

QAnon has infected mainstream politics. Indeed, some 11 congressional candidates, all running as Republicans, were on the ballot in 2020.[45] Social media is not the only source of such conspiracies, as FOX news has also elevated such theories—again, taking the paranoia much farther than Hofstadter imagined. In a conversation with President Trump's son, Eric, FOX news commentator asked, "Q can do some crazy stuff with the pizza stuff and the Wayfair stuff, but they've also uncovered a lot of great stuff when it comes to [Jeffrey] Epstein and when it comes to the Deep State. I never saw Q as dangerous as ANTIFA. But ANTIFA gets to run wild on the Internet. What do you think? What's going on there?"[46]

During COVID-19 lockdowns, QAnon theories spread, as Internet searches were up. Data from Google showed an increase in searches for "adenochrome" which *Mother Jones* explains is, "in line with the conspiracy's belief that elites use the blood of children to create adrenochrome, a therapeutically injected chemical compound."[47] QAnon believers also spread the belief that the COVID-19 pandemic was a "deep state" hoax, that masks were unnecessary, and a variety of other outlandish claims about the origin of the virus. Many used the hashtag #COVID911 and warned that the "plandemic" was meant to ruin Trump's reelection chances. For example, one YouTube video that garnered 800,000 views declared:

> In 2015, as directed by the globalist criminal corruption network known as the deep state President Barack Obama authorized millions in funding for the Wuhan Institute of Virology, the location now understood to be the epicenter of the COVID-19 outbreak. The research carried out here was to provide the agent for a global biological attack on a scale never before seen, one that would be timed for release within an election year.[48]

The video was uploaded many times and now contains a warning from YouTube, but viewers need only click through to watch it.[49]

Why should we care if people believe in conspiracy theories? Despite being works of fiction, conspiracy theories have real-world consequences. The believers themselves are negatively impacted. For example, believing COVID-19 to be a hoax or a "scamdemic" can lead the believer to take risky actions, jeopardizing their health and the health of those around them. Arkansas state Senator Jason Rapert tested positive for COVID-19 after posting to Facebook an article calling the virus a hoax and he said a mask mandate is "…an overreach of executive power."[50] Another such believer, Tony Green, wrote:

> I admit traveling deep into the conspiracy trap over COVID-19. All the defiant behavior of Trump's more radical and rowdy cult followers, I participated in it. I was a hard-ass that stood up for my "God-given rights." In great haste, I began prognosticating the alphabet soup about this "scamdemic." I believed the virus to be a hoax. I believed the mainstream media and the Democrats were using it to create panic, crash the economy and destroy Trump's chances at re-election.[51]

He goes on to detail how he, along with many of his family members, got sick after a gathering he hosted. In heartbreaking detail, he describes a family member's death and funeral.[52]

Besides the impact on believers, we have seen that conspiracy theories traumatize and cause further anguish to victims and their families who become the objects of harassment by conspiracists. Such was the case for the parents and families of victims, as well as survivors, of mass shootings. Moreover, conspiracy theories that put forward a narrative about "crisis actors" and "false flag" attacks after mass shootings serve to muddy the waters in the debate over meaningful gun reforms.

Conspiracy theories motivates violence. The FBI has issued a bulletin that warns, "conspiracy theory-driven domestic extremists ...such as QANON adherents represent a potential domestic terrorism threat."[53] It goes on to explain:

> One key assumption driving these assessments is that certain conspiracy theory narratives tacitly support or legitimize violent action. The FBI also assumes some, but not all individuals or domestic extremists who hold such beliefs will act on them. The FBI assesses these conspiracy theories very likely will emerge, spread, and evolve in the modem information marketplace, occasionally driving both groups and individual extremists to carry out criminal or violent acts.[54]

The FBI then lists a number of incidents motivated by a range of conspiracy theories, including those promoted by politicians, and amplified by right-wing media personalities, that resulted in arrests and convictions of the conspiracists who acted on their beliefs.

The widespread belief in conspiracy theories causes a fraying in the social fabric, sowing distrust in institutions and leaders. It poisons the electorate and threatens democracy itself. Political scientists have long documented the electorate's lack of knowledge.[55] Democratic theorists concern themselves with whether a democracy could be healthy and sustained when voters lived in ignorance. Scholars point out that voters need not be fully versed on the issues of the day, and that "low information" voting can still result in a reasonable decision at the polls.[56] However, these theories were posited before the post-truth reality we now find ourselves in. From President Trump's frequent refrain of "fake news" to the barrage of conspiracy theories on social media, there has been a noticeable decay in democratic discourse and there is a very real threat of further withering of the norms and values that define America's grand experiment in democracy. It is no wonder that the work of Hannah Arendt's work on totalitarianism and George Orwell's *1984* have been flying of the shelves in the age of Trump and QAnon.[57]

## Notes

1 Following Michael Barkun, we define a conspiracy theory as "...the belief that an organization made up of individuals or groups was or is acting covertly to achieve some malevolent end." Barkun 2013.
2 Feldman 2017.
3 Levin, October 2, 2017.
4 For a thorough summary of Jones' many claims, see "Alex Jones' week of irresponsible Las Vegas shooting conspiracy theories: Jones has recklessly

accused a multitude of people and groups of being involved in the worst mass shooting in modern U.S. history," by Timothy Johnson, reporting for Media Matters. His report also links to the video clips. See Johnson 2017.
5 The Alex Jones Show 2017.
6 Sanford 2017.
7 Levin, October 2, 2017.
8 Levin, October 26, 2017.
9 Silverstein 2018.
10 Koebler 2018.
11 Concettafannin2 2012.
12 In 2019, Alex Jones retracted his claims, as a result of a lawsuit brought against him by the parents of the victims. For an overview, see "Alex Jones blames 'psychosis' for his Sandy Hook conspiracies" by Amanda Sakuma, 2019, in Vox. See Sakuma 2019.
13 Associated Press, 2019.
14 NPR 2019.
15 Allen 2020.
16 Peyser 2018.
17 Graham 2018.
18 CNN 2018.
19 Grunberger 2018.
20 Doubek 2018.
21 Bader et al. 2020.
22 Jamil and Rousseau, 2011.
23 Douglas et al. 2017.
24 Goertzel 1994.
25 Goertzel 1994.
26 Douglas, Sutton, and Cichocka 2017.
27 Swami et al. 2014.
28 Douglas et al. 2016.
29 Prooijen and Acker, 2015.
30 Douglas et al. 2016.
31 Sunstein and Vermeule, 2008.
32 Wood et al. 2012.
33 Lantian et al. 2017.
34 Douglas et al. 2017.
35 Douglas et al. 2016.
36 Ibid.
37 Ibid.
38 Lantian et al. 2017.
39 Sunstein and Vermeule, 2008.
40 Ibid.
41 Lopez 2016.
42 Hofstadter 1963.
43 Ibid.
44 Sommer 2020.
45 Knutson 2020.
46 Wade and Wade 2020.
47 Breland and Rangarajan 2020.
48 The Associated Press 2020.

49 StormIsUponUs 2020.
50 Crump 2020.
51 Green 2020.
52 Ibid.
53 Winter 2019.
54 Federal Bureau of Investigation 2019.
55 For example, see Carpini and Keeter, 1996.
56 Popkin 1994.
57 Associated Press, 2017.

## Bibliography

The Alex Jones Show. "The Alex Jones Show 10/04/2017." Video. 2017. https://www.mediamatters.org/embed/clips/2017:10:05:56315:gcn-thealexjoneshow-20171004-brother. Accessed August 5, 2020.

Allen, Karma. *"Sandy Hook Shooting 'Conspiracy Theorist' Arrested after Tormenting Families of Victims: Police."* ABC News, January 27, 2020. https://abcnews.go.com/US/sandy-hook-shooting-conspiracy-theorist-arrested-tormenting-families/story?id=68570486. Accessed August 5, 2020.

Associated Press. *"'Nobody Died at Sandy Hook' Publisher Apologizes to Dad of Murdered Boy."* CBS News, June 18, 2019. https://www.cbsnews.com/news/sandy-hook-lawsuit-lenny-pozner-father-of-boy-killed-wins-defamation-suit/. Accessed August 5, 2020.

Associated Press. *"Sales of Orwell's Dystopian Classic '1984' Soar After Trump Claims, 'Alternative Facts.'"* NBC News, January 25, 2017. https://www.nbcnews.com/business/consumer/sales-orwell-s-dystopian-classic-1984-soar-after-trump-claims-n711951. Accessed August 5, 2020. Associated Press. *"Video Stitches False Claims Together to Paint COVID-19 as a Political Hoax."* July 9, 2020. https://apnews.com/afs:Content:9065413346. Accessed August 5, 2020.

Bader, Christopher D., Joseph O. Baker, L. Edward Day, and Ann Gordon. *Fear Itself: The Causes and Consequences of Fear in America.* New York: NYU Press, 2020.

Barkun, Michael. *A Culture of Conspiracy: Apocalyptic Visions in Contemporary America.* 2nd ed. Berkeley: University of California Press, 2013.

Breland, Ali, and Sinduja Rangarajan. "How the Coronavirus Spread QAnon." *Mother Jones,* June 23, 2020. https://www.motherjones.com/politics/2020/06/qanon-coronavirus/. Accessed August 5, 2020.

Carpini, Michael X. Delli, and Scott Keeter. *What Americans Know about Politics and Why It Matters.* London: Yale University Press, 1996.

CNN. *"Shooting Survivor: I'm Not a Crisis Actor."* 2018. https://www.cnn.com/videos/politics/2018/02/21/david-hogg-reaction-don-jr-like-tweet-school-shooting-ac-sot.cnn. Accessed August 5, 2020.

Concettafannin2. *"The Sandy Hook Massacre: Unanswered Questions and Missing Information."* Memory Hole Blog, December 24, 2012. http://memoryholeblog.org/2012/12/24/the-sandy-hook-massacre-unanswered-questions-and-missing-information/. Accessed August 5, 2020.

Crump, James. *"Anti-Mask US State Senator Who Called Coronavirus a Hoax Tests Positive for Covid-19."* Independent, July 27, 2020. https://www.independent.co.uk/news/

world/americas/us-politics/jason-rapert-coronavirus-hoax-face-mask-arkansas-asa-hutchinson-a9640156.html. Accessed August 5, 2020.

Doubek, James. "*Advertisers Ditch Laura Ingraham after She Mocks Parkland Activist.*" *NPR*, March 30, 2018. https://www.npr.org/sections/thetwo-way/2018/03/30/598194392/advertisers-ditch-laura-ingraham-after-she-mocks-parkland-activist. Accessed August 5, 2020.

Douglas, Karen M., Robbie M. Sutton, Mitchell J. Callan, Rael J. Dawtry, and Annelie J. Harvey. "Someone Is Pulling the Strings: Hypersensitive Agency Detection and Belief in Conspiracy Theories." *Thinking & Reasoning 22*, no. 1 (2016): 57–77. https://doi.org/10.1080/13546783.2015.1051586.

Douglas, Karen M., Robbie M. Sutton, and Aleksandra Cichocka. "The Psychology of Conspiracy Theories." *Current Directions in Psychological Science 26*, no. 6 (December 7, 2017): 538–542. https://doi.org/10.1177/0963721417718261.

Federal Bureau of Investigation. "*FBI Conspiracy Theory Redacted.*" *FBI Phoenix Field Office*, May 30, 2019. https://www.scribd.com/document/420379775/FBI-Conspiracy-Theory-Redacted. Accessed August 5, 2020.

Feldman, Brian. "*The Vicious Circle of 4chan's Mass-Shooting Hoaxes.*" *Intelligencer*, October 2, 2017. https://nymag.com/intelligencer/2017/10/the-vicious-circle-of-4chans-mass-shooting-hoaxes.html. Accessed August 5, 2020.

Goertzel, Ted. "Belief in Conspiracy Theories." *Political Psychology 15*, no. 4 (December 1994): 731–742. https://doi.org/10.2307/3791630.

Graham, Jefferson. "'*Crisis Actors' YouTube Video Removed after It Tops 'Trending' Videos.*" *USA Today*, February 21, 2018. https://www.usatoday.com/story/tech/talkingtech/2018/02/21/crisis-actors-youtube-david-hogg-video-removed-after-tops-trending-video/360107002/.

Green, Tony. "*A Harsh Lesson in the Reality of COVID-19.*" *Dallas Voice*, July 24, 2020. https://dallasvoice.com/a-harsh-lesson-in-the-reality-of-covid-19/. Accessed August 5, 2020.

Grunberger, Alessia. "*Ted Nugent Calls Parkland Survivors 'Liars.'*" *CNN*, April 2, 2018. https://www.cnn.com/2018/03/31/politics/nra-member-calls-parkland-survivors-liars/index.html. Accessed August 5, 2020.

Hofstadter, Richard. *The Paranoid Style in American Politics and Other Essays*. Cambridge, Massachusetts: Harvard University Press, 1963, pp. 29–30.

Jamil, Uzma, and Cécile Rousseau. "Challenging the 'Official' Story of 9/11: Community Narratives and Conspiracy Theories." *Ethnicities 11*, no. 2 (June 7, 2011): 245–261. https://doi.org/10.1177/1468796811398836.

Johnson, Timothy. "*Alex Jones' Week of Las Vegas Shooting Conspiracy Theories.*" *Media Matters for America*, October 6, 2017. https://www.mediamatters.org/alex-jones/alex-jones-week-irresponsible-las-vegas-shooting-conspiracy-theories. Accessed August 5, 2020.

Knutson, Jacob. "*11 Republican Congressional Nominees Support the QAnon Conspiracy Theory.*" *Axios*, July 12, 2020. https://www.axios.com/qanon-nominees-congress-gop-8086ed21-b7d3-46af-9016-d132e65ba801.html. Accessed August 5, 2020.

Koebler, Jason. "*Where the 'Crisis Actor' Conspiracy Theory Comes From.*" *Vice*, February 22, 2018. https://www.vice.com/en_us/article/pammy8/what-is-a-crisis-actor-conspiracy-theory-explanation-parkland-shooting-sandy-hook. Accessed August 5, 2020.

Lantian, Anthony, Dominique Muller, Cécile Nurra, and Karen M. Douglas. "'I Know Things They Don't Know!'" *Social Psychology 48*, no. 3 (July 1, 2017): 160–173. https://doi.org/10.1027/1864-9335/a000306.

Levin, Sam. "*Facebook and Google Promote Politicized Fake News about Las Vegas Shooter.*" *The Guardian*, October 2, 2017. https://www.theguardian.com/us-news/2017/oct/02/las-vegas-shooting-facebook-google-fake-news-shooter. Accessed August 5, 2020.

Levin, Sam. "*'I Hope Someone Truly Shoots You': Online Conspiracy Theorists Harass Vegas Victims.*" *The Guardian*, October 26, 2017. https://www.theguardian.com/us-news/2017/oct/26/las-vegas-shooting-conspiracy-theories-social-media. Accessed August 5, 2020.

Lopez, German. "*Pizzagate, the Totally False Conspiracy Theory That Led a Gunman to a DC Pizzeria, Explained.*" *Vox*, December 5, 2016. https://www.vox.com/policy-and-politics/2016/12/5/13842258/pizzagate-comet-ping-pong-fake-news. Accessed August 5, 2020.

NPR. *His Son Was Killed at Sandy Hook. Then Came the Online Harassment.* December 14, 2019. https://www.npr.org/2019/12/14/788117375/his-son-was-killed-at-sandy-hook-then-came-the-online-harassment. Accessed August 5, 2020.

Peyser, Eve. "*Right-Wing Talking Heads Are Smearing the Parkland Survivors.*" *Vice*, February 21, 2018. https://www.vice.com/en_us/article/bj5yqw/rush-limbaugh-ted-nugent-parkland. Accessed August 5, 2020.

Popkin, Samuel L. *The Reasoning Voter: Communication and Persuasion in Political Campaigns.* 2nd ed. Chicago: The University of Chicago Press, 1994.

Prooijen, Jan-Willem van, and Michele Acker. "The Influence of Control on Belief in Conspiracy Theories: Conceptual and Applied Extensions." *Applied Cognitive Psychology 29*, no. 5 (August 10, 2015): 753–761. https://doi.org/10.1002/acp.3161.

Sakuma, Amanda. "*Alex Jones Blames 'Psychosis' for His Sandy Hook Conspiracies.*" *Vox*, March 31, 2019. https://www.vox.com/2019/3/31/18289271/alex-jones-psychosis-conspiracies-sandy-hook-hoax. Accessed August 5, 2020.

Sanford, George. "*Las Vegas Massacre—Staged Crisis Actors—False Flag.*" 153News.net video, December 6, 2017. Accessed August 5, 2020. http://153news.net/watch_video.php?v=UGKAU4ONS8G6.

Silverstein, Jason. "*Las Vegas Shooting: One Year Later, Hundreds of Videos Traumatize Some Survivors.*" *CBS News*, October 1, 2018. https://www.cbsnews.com/news/las-vegas-shooting-one-year-later-hundreds-of-online-videos-traumatize-survivors/. Accessed August 5, 2020.

Sommer, Will. "*Trump Throws Fresh Fuel on Dangerous QAnon Conspiracy Theory.*" *Daily Beast*, January 2, 2020. https://www.thedailybeast.com/trump-throws-fresh-fuel-on-dangerous-qanon-conspiracy-theory. Accessed August 5, 2020.

StormIsUponUs. "*Covid911 – INSURGENCY.*" YouTube video, 2020. Accessed August 5, 2020. https://www.youtube.com/watch?v=5smALFZgvUM&bpctr=1595890977.

Sunstein, Cass R., and Adrian Vermeule. "*Conspiracy Theories.*" *SSRN Scholarly Paper*, January 15, 2008. https://papers.ssrn.com/abstract=1084585.

Swami, Viren, Martin Voracek, Stefan Stieger, Ulrich S. Tran, and Adrian Furnham. "Analytic Thinking Reduces Belief in Conspiracy Theories." *Cognition 133*, no. 3 (December 2014): 572–585. https://doi.org/10.1016/j.cognition.2014.08.006.

Wade, Peter. "*Fox News Touting QAnon Is All You Need to Know about the So-Called 'News' Network.*" *Rolling Stone*, July 26, 2020. https://www.rollingstone.com/politics/politics-news/fox-news-jesse-watters-touts-qanon-1034136/. Accessed August 5, 2020.

Winter, Dana. "*Exclusive: FBI Document Warns Conspiracy Theories Are a New Domestic Terrorism Threat.*" *Yahoo News*, August 1, 2019. https://news.yahoo.com/fbi-documents-conspiracy-theories-terrorism-160000507.html. Accessed August 5, 2020.

Wood, Michael J., Karen M. Douglas, and Robbie M. Sutton. "Dead and Alive: Beliefs in Contradictory Conspiracy Theories." *Social Psychological and Personality Science 3*, no. 6 (November 1, 2012): 767–773. https://doi.org/10.1177/1948550611434786.

# 5 Conclusion

*Ann Gordon and Kai Hamilton-Gentry*

Insecurity and fear are widespread in America. As we have observed throughout this volume, Americans are afraid of terror attacks in their homeland and of personally being the victim of a mass or random shooting. Indeed, fear of mass shootings has been the fastest-growing fear in America, as measured by 5 years of data from the Chapman Survey of American Fears. These fears are fueled are by conspiracy theories that confuse and frighten America, as they have crept from the fringes and into the mainstream.

There is a growing threat from domestic terrorists whose mass shootings are tied to white supremacist ideology that promotes fear of immigrants, Jews, Muslims, and Blacks that has motivated shootings from El Paso, Texas, to Pittsburgh, Pennsylvania, to Christchurch, New Zealand, and Charleston, South Carolina. In Chapter 2, we explored how the fear of Muslims and the wrongheaded association of a religion with terrorism leads to targeting Muslims. It has led to the violation of civil liberties when innocent people are swept up in the "See Something, Say Something Campaign®," because members of the public submit erroneous leads that grow from prejudice, rather than from observations of potential indicators or behaviors that constitute precursors to terrorism. Moreover, the nature of threat, and who is considered a terrorist, is contingent upon partisanship and even media habits. Chapter 2 emphasizes public education on what constitutes a threat and awareness of pre-incident indicators as a way to improve the public's ability to assist law enforcement in countering violent extremism.

The threat posed by white supremacists and hate-filled terror groups eclipses that of foreign terrorist organizations, though they remain an active threat. As FBI Director Christopher Wray told the House Judiciary Committee:

> … domestic violent extremists collectively pose a steady threat of violence and economic harm to the United States. Trends may

shift, but the underlying drivers for domestic violent extremism—such as perceptions of government or law enforcement overreach, socio-political conditions, racism, anti-Semitism, Islamophobia, and reactions to legislative actions—remain constant. The FBI is most concerned about lone offender attacks, primarily shootings, as they have served as the dominant lethal mode for domestic violent extremist attacks. More deaths were caused by domestic violent extremists than international terrorists in recent years.[1]

The top threat we face from domestic violent extremists stems from those we now identify as racially/ethnically motivated violent extremists (RMVEs). RMVEs were the primary source of ideologically motivated lethal incidents and violence in 2018 and 2019, and have been considered the most lethal of all domestic extremism movements since 2001.[2]

One manifestation of right-wing violent extremism, associated with the term "Boogaloo," grew and flourished during COVID-19 lockdowns. One study found that Boogaloo extremists, who are eager to touch off a new civil war, used Facebook to organize. The analysis looked at 125 Boogaloo Facebook groups:

> More than 60% of the groups were created in the last three months, as Covid-19 quarantines took hold in the U.S., and they've attracted tens of thousands of members in the last 30 days. In several private boogaloo Facebook groups...members discussed tactical strategies, combat medicine, and various types of weapons, including how to develop explosives and the merits of using flame throwers. Some members appeared to take inspiration from President Donald Trump's recent tweets calling on people to "liberate" states where governors have imposed stay-at-home orders.[3]

The Boogaloo movement has used the pandemic to grow its membership by recruiting at anti-mask and anti-lockdown rallies, where resentment of government runs high.[4] Taking their name from the movie *Breakin 2': Electric Boogaloo*, with the notion of bringing about a second civil war, the groups favor aloha print shirts that are a reference to the "big luau," which is another version of the Boogaloo. The Southern Poverty Law Center explains the origins and meaning as originating about a decade ago:

> The boogaloo meme itself emerged concurrently in antigovernment and white power online spaces in the early 2010s. In both of these communities, "boogaloo" was frequently associated with racist violence and, in many cases, was an explicit call for race war. Today the

term is regularly deployed by white nationalists and neo-Nazis who want to see society descend into chaos so that they can come to power and build a new fascist state.[5]

Boogaloo violence has already begun. In Colorado, a man espousing Boogaloo ideas, was arrested in a bombing plot. He had recently testified in the state capitol in opposition to the state's red flag law.[6] Prior to his arrest, the man had published a manifesto online, calling for "armed defiance against tyrants."[7] Three men were arrested in Nevada for their bombing plots that targeted protestors at ReOpen rallies, as well as BLM protests, in an effort to provoke violent confrontation between protestors and police.[8] Two men were arrested after shooting and killing one federal officer and wounding another in Oakland and then killing a Santa Cruz County sheriff's deputy 8 days later.[9] The shooter had posted to Facebook: "Go to the riots and support our own cause. Show them the real targets. Use their anger to fuel our fire. Think outside the box. We have mobs of angry people to use to our advantage." A boogaloo patch was recovered from the van that he used that day. A suspected accomplice was also arrested after confessing to the FBI.[10]

In case there was any doubt as to his intentions, the shooter also used his own blood to write "BOOG" and "I became unreasonable" and "stop the duopoly" on the hood of a hijacked car, a picture of which was included in the criminal complaint.[11]

Alarmingly, gun manufacturers have been marketing to Boogaloo members. Moreover, Facebook and Instagram ran ads promoting products marketed to Boogaloo supporters, such as aloha print body armor.[12] Although Facebook announced that they we were designating Boogaloo content as emanating from a "dangerous organization" and say, "For months, we have removed boogaloo content when there is a clear connection to violence or a credible threat to public safety, and today's designation will mean we remove more content going forward..."[13] such material is still circulating on the Internet.[14]

Fear fuels gun purchases in times of upheaval, such as the COVID-19 pandemic that made it seem like the whole world had come to a screeching halt (though not gun stores in many American states). Fear of changes in gun laws also leads to more purchases. The increase of guns in circulation inevitably leads to more deaths (see Chapter 3). As gun violence has risen, so too has the fear of being the victim of a mass or random shooting, in a seemingly never-ending cycle.

In tandem with the rise in fear over possible gun regulation following events such as mass shootings—particularly those that receive the most media attention—comes the creation and spread of conspiracy theories.

As we have recounted, these bizarre and fictional theories have real-world consequences, from traumatizing victims and their families all over again to spurring fresh violence.

We have examined some proposed solutions to curb gun violence in Chapter 3, such as universal background checks, extreme risk protection orders, and banning assault weapons and high-capacity magazines, among others. A big obstacle to achieving these solutions is overcoming fear and defeating those that stoke fears, such as the NRA and right-wing conspiracy theorists.

## Pop Culture and Media Coverage of Mass Shootings

As a society, we must reject turning the tragedy of school shootings into pop culture objects and refuse to grant shooters notoriety. Glorifying the attacks serves to perpetuate and even normalize such violence. For example, one clothing designer debuted school-shooting-themed hoodies during their New York Fashion week show. As CNN reports, the hoodies were part of the brand's spring/summer 2020 collection and were emblazoned with "Stoneman Douglas," "Sandy Hook," "Virginia Tech," and "Columbine."[15] This is even more alarming when one considers that school shooters are often "fans" of earlier school shooters and they join "fan communities." Jaclyn Schildkraut and H. Jaymi Elsass have explained, "Each shooting has its own dedicated group of followers. One of the largest groups is the Columbiners, named after the 1999 attack...."[16] They go on to point out that the followers range from aspiring school shooters to people who feel suicidal or homicidal, and even fans who want to date school shooters.

After the 2012 shooting in Aurora, Colorado, a campaign called "No Notoriety" was born and has been embraced by Parkland survivors and their families. The father of one victim, Alex Teves, has attempted to shift the narrative from the shooter to the victims.[17] He notes that this should not interrupt dissemination of useful and relevant information. Rather, the campaign focuses on limiting the use of the perpetrator's name over the course of media coverage. They stress a singular and intentional use of the perpetrator's name in an effort to minimize the individual attention that is given to the shooter, and shifts focus to the situation as a whole. Media coverage does little to minimize copycat shootings and through the traditional sensationalization of the event, disturbed subcultures are fueled, violent behavior is normalized, and something akin to a "fan base" is developed in the process.

Days after a video of the Parkland shooter circulated on the Internet, survivor Emma Gonzalez wrote in a tweet, "I've been off twitter for a couple days. First thing I see when I log back in is the person who killed my friends. Please do us a favor and Listen to us when we say we don't want his Fucking Face plastered everywhere we look; thank you have a good night because none of us will be."[18]

The shooter wanted attention and got what he wanted after his picture, name, and video manifesto were released to the public.[19,20] In the video, he discussed his premeditated crimes and said, "When you see me on the news, you'll know who I am." Since then, the Parkland shooter has received fan mail. As of March 2018, he had received anywhere from 100–200 pieces of mail from men, women, and girls from all over the world.[21] Some contained sexually suggestive photos and others are filled with sympathetic writings from people who believe they can fix him or console him. Had his name not been plastered across media sources, it's likely he would not receive these letters that give him the validation he was so desperately seeking.[22,23]

The media's role in incidents like these should be to minimize harm done while providing relevant information to the public rather than sensationalizing issues and giving attention to the shooter rather than the victims of the event. Infamy is a motivation for some individuals and can be a source of motivation for copycat criminals who receive a constant stream of information from the media. This is evidenced in the Virginia Tech massacre in which the shooter idolized the perpetrators of the Columbine High School shooting.[24] The same thing happened at Sandy Hook and most recently in the mosque attacks in Christchurch, New Zealand. The overwhelming difference in this case is that Prime Minister Jacinda Ardern refuses to release information about the shooter. She said, "He sought so many things from his act of terror, but one was notoriety. And that is why you will never hear me mention his name. He is a terrorist. He is a criminal. He is an extremist. But he will, when I speak, be nameless." University of Alabama Professor Adam Lankford notes that between 1966 and 2015, he found 24 cases of mass shootings in which perpetrators mentioned media coverage and fame as some of the main motivators behind their actions.[25] Instead, the "No Notoriety" campaign suggests focus should be on the victims of the shooting and should not give attention-seeking extremists what they want.

The media must also avoid the amplification of conspiracy theories that surround mass shootings. As we saw in Chapter 4, such theories proliferate on a variety of platforms from television to social media sites like YouTube, Facebook, and Reddit. These damaging lies circulate widely. Moreover, they do real harm to victims and their families, particularly when these online conspiracy theories lead to real-world harassment and even violence.

## Looking to the Future

One cannot discount the potential for a rise in gun violence, mass shootings, and attacks in the near future. As we have pointed out, there are more guns than ever in circulation, due to panic buying tied to fear during the COVID-19 pandemic.[26] Heavily armed right-wing extremists have been calling for a civil war and have already begun acting on their threats.[27] As schools reopen, there is also the terrifying prospect of seeing the return of school shootings. Even as schools take on the herculean task of holding classes during a pandemic, they must be vigilant for the signs that could indicate a potential attack.

Despite these sobering thoughts, we can see reason for optimism. A new generation is rising and leading the way through their activism. From the Parkland teens to the Black Lives Matter movement, and the teens who raised money to equip every school in their district with bleeding control kits, Gen Z is not content with the status quo. Gen Z is more racially and ethnically diverse than previous generations, more educated, and more adept than any generation before at leveraging social media to organize for change.[28] Gen Z activism is inclusive and embraces intersectionality.[29] Gen Z is out in front of the Black Lives Matter protests, more so than any other age group.[30] Their activism addresses a range of issues from climate change and immigration to systemic racism and gun violence. As survivor Tanzil Phillip said to lawmakers, 1 week after the shooting at Marjory Stoneman Douglas High School, "We are here, our voices are loud, and we're not stopping until change happens."[31] This generation promises change—and from what they have already accomplished—they will deliver.

## Notes

1 Wray 2020.
2 Wray 2020.
3 Tech Transparency Project 2020.
4 Owen 2020.
5 Miller 2020.
6 Sallinger 2020.
7 Jojola 2020.
8 Dickson 2020.
9 Woodlard 2020.
10 Karbal 2020.
11 Woodlard 2020.
12 Mac 2020.
13 Facebook 2020.
14 Hoplitearmor 2019 and "Hoplite Armor" 2019. See, for example, this Instagram post "Be ready with the Hoplite Armor Aloha Combat Shirt and Plate Carrier." One comment on the post read, "Did y'all just make a joke

about the #boogaloo = #aloha #winnersneverquit #partyondudes #beexcellenttoeachother #freedom #furearms #bodyarmor #selfdefense #murica #platecarrier #combatshirt #alohacombatshirt #alohaplatecarrier #ohana #mahalo"
15 Dixon 2019.
16 Schildkraut and Elsass 2016.
17 Beckett 2018.
18 Emma González (@Emma4Change), "I've been off twitter for a couple days. First thing I see when I log back in is the person who killed my friends. Please do us a favor and Listen to us when we say we don't want his Fucking Face plastered everywhere we look, thank you have a good night because none of us will be," Twitter, May 30, 2018, https://twitter.com/Emma4Change/status/1001990541276536833.
19 Robles 2018.
20 Chuck, Johnson, and Siemaszko 2018.
21 Flores 2018.
22 Berman and Eltagouri 2018.
23 Tribune News Service 2019.
24 Associated Press 2007.
25 Kwong 2019.
26 Beckett 2020.
27 Associated Press 2020; Department of Justice 2020; Gartrell 2020.
28 Parker and Igielnik 2020.
29 Mejia 2018.
30 Barroso and Minkin 2020.
31 Burke 2018.

## Bibliography

Associated Press. "Cho Idolized Columbine Killers." Denver Post, April 18, 2007. https://www.denverpost.com/2007/04/18/cho-idolized-columbine-killers/. Accessed August 4, 2020.

Associated Press. "Man with Links to 'Boogaloo' Movement Indicted in Texas." U.S. News, June 12, 2020. https://www.usnews.com/news/us/articles/2020-06-12/man-with-links-to-boogaloo-movement-indicted-in-texas. Accessed August 4, 2020.

Barroso, Amanda, and Rachel Minkin. "Recent Protest Attendees Are More Eacially and Ethnically Diverse, Younger than Americans Overall." Pew Research Center, June 24, 2020. https://www.pewresearch.org/fact-tank/2020/06/24/recent-protest-attendees-are-more-racially-and-ethnically-diverse-younger-than-americans-overall/. Accessed August 4, 2020.

Beckett, Lois. "Americans Purchasing Record-Breaking Numbers of Guns amid Coronavirus." The Guardian, April 1, 2020. https://www.theguardian.com/world/2020/apr/01/us-gun-purchases-coronavirus-record. Accessed December 6, 2020.

Beckett, Lois. "'No Notoriety': the Campaign to Focus on Shooting Victims, Not Killers." The Guardian, July 7, 2018. https://www.theguardian.com/us-news/2018/jul/07/no-notoriety-media-focus-victims-shooter. Accessed August 4, 2020.

Berman, Mark, and Marwa Eltagouri. "Parkland Suspect Detailed Plans in Chilling Videos: 'I'm Going to Be the Next School Shooter.'" Washington Post, May 30, 2018. https://www.washingtonpost.com/news/post-nation/wp/2018/05/30/parkland-shooting-suspect-detailed-plans-in-videos-im-going-to-be-the-next-school-shooter/. Accessed August 4, 2020.

Burke, Peter. "Marjory Stoneman Douglas High School Students Give Impassioned Speeches in Tallahassee." Local10.com, February 21, 2018. https://www.local10.com/news/2018/02/21/marjory-stoneman-douglas-high-school-students-give-impassioned-speeches-in-tallahassee/. Accessed August 4, 2020.

Chuck, Elizabeth, Alex Johnson, and Corky Siemaszko. "17 Killed in Mass Shooting at High School in Parkland, Florida." NBCNews, December 14, 2018. https://www.nbcnews.com/news/us-news/police-respond-shooting-parkland-florida-high-school-n848101. Accessed August 4, 2020.

Department of Justice. "Federal Grand Jury Indicts Three Men for seeking to Exploit Protests in Las Vegas and Incite Violence June 17, 2020. https://www.justice.gov/usao-nv/pr/federal-grand-jury-indicts-three-men-seeking-exploit-protests-las-vegas-and-incite. Accessed August 4, 2020.

Dickson, Caitlin. "'Boogaloo' Arrests in Nevada Portray Extremists Using Protests to Incite Civil War." Yahoo!, June 5, 2020. https://news.yahoo.com/boogaloo-arrests-in-nevada-portray-extremists-using-protests-to-incite-civil-war-131125733.html. Accessed August 4, 2020.

Dixon, Emily. "Aloha Line." *Hoplite Armor Store*, September 18, 2019. https://www.hoplitearmor.com/collections/aloha-line. Accessed August 4, 2020.

Facebook. "Banning a Violent Network in the US." June 30, 2020. https://about.fb.com/news/2020/06/banning-a-violent-network-in-the-us/. Accessed August 4, 2020.

Flores, Rosa. "The Amount of Fan Mail the Parkland Shooter Is Receiving Is Unreal." CNN, March 30, 2018. https://www.cnn.com/2018/03/29/us/nikolas-cruz-prison-fan-mail-trnd/index.html. Accessed August 4, 2020.

Gartrell, Nate. "California Men Who Officials Say Met on 'Boogaloo' Group Indicted in Officer's Killing." The Sacramento Bee, June 29, 2020. https://www.sacbee.com/news/california/article243881047.html. Accessed August 4, 2020.

Hoplitearmor. "Be Ready with the Hoplite Armor Aloha Combat Shirt and Plate Carrier." Instagram, September 29, 2019. https://www.instagram.com/p/B3AD0O7AE_a/?hl=en. Accessed August 4, 2020; site inactive on December 6, 2020.

Jojola, Jeremy. "Pipe Bomb Suspect's Family Says He's Too Dangerous to Be Free." KUSA-TV, May 9, 2020. https://www.9news.com/article/news/investigations/pipe-bomb-suspects-family-manifesto/73-fc065448-226b-4124-ad2d-98f0ed2806b9. Accessed August 4, 2020.

Karbal, Ian. "'Boogaloo' Believers Think a Civil War Is Coming. These Gun Firms Are Openly Marketing to Them." The Trace, June 29, 2020. https://www.thetrace.org/2020/06/boogaloo-gun-ammunition-marketing-facebook-instagram/. Accessed August 4, 2020.

Kwong, Matt. "The Case for Denying Mass Killers Fame in Order to Fight the Deadly 'Contagion Effect.'" CBC, March 20, 2019. https://www.scmp.com/news/world/united-states-canada/article/3005353/parkland-school-shooter-nikolas-cruz-writes. Accessed August 4, 2020.

Mac, Ryan. "Facebook Has Been Profiting from Boogaloo Ads Promoting Civil War and Unrest." BuzzFeed News, July 2, 2020. https://www.buzzfeednews.com/article/ryanmac/facebook-instagram-profit-boogaloo-ads. Accessed August 4, 2020.

Mejia, Zameena. "3 reasons Gen Z activists have changed the gun control conversation when no one else could." CNBC, March 14, 2018. https://www.cnbc.com/2018/03/14/how-gen-z-activists-have-changed-the-conversation-around-guns.html. Accessed August 4, 2020.

Miller, Cassie. "The 'Boogaloo' Started as a Racist Meme." Southern Poverty Law Cente, June 5, 2020. https://www.splcenter.org/hatewatch/2020/06/05/boogaloo-started-racist-meme. Accessed August 4, 2020.

Owen, Tess. "The 'Boogaloo Bois' Are Bringing Their AR-15s and Civil War Ideology to the Lockdown Protests." Vice, May 8, 2020. https://www.vice.com/en_us/article/y3zmj5/the-boogaloo-bois-are-bringing-their-ar-15s-and-civil-war-ideology-to-the-lockdown-protests. Accessed August 4, 2020.

Parker, Kim, and Ruth Igielnik. "On the Cusp of Adulthood and Facing an Uncertain Future: We Know about Gen Z So Far." Pew Research Cetner, May 14, 2020. https://www.pewsocialtrends.org/essay/on-the-cusp-of-adulthood-and-facing-an-uncertain-future-what-we-know-about-gen-z-so-far/. Accessed August 4, 2020.

Robles, Frances. "'You'll All Know Who I Am,' Parkland Suspect Said in Video." The New York Times, May 30, 2018. https://www.nytimes.com/2018/05/30/us/nikolas-cruz-parkland-video.html. Accessed August 4, 2020.

Tribune News Service. "Parkland School Shooter Nikolas Cruz Writes Disturbing Love Letters from Jail to 'Miley': I Want to Name My Sons after Guns." April 9, 2019. South China Morning Post. https://www.scmp.com/news/world/united-states-canada/article/3005353/parkland-school-shooter-nikolas-cruz-writes. Accessed August 4, 2020.

Sallinger, Rick. "Bradley Bunn, Loveland Man Arrested after FBI Finds Pipe Bombs, Testified against Red Flag Law." CBS Denver, May 5, 2020. https://denver.cbslocal.com/2020/05/05/bradley-bunn-loveland-fbi-pipe-bombs/. Accessed August 4, 2020.

Schildkraut, Jaclyn, and Jaymi Elsass. Mass Shootings: Media, Myths, and Realities. Santa Barbara, CA: Praeger, 2016.

Tech Transparency Project. "Extremists Are Using Facebook to Organize for Civil War amid Coronavirus." May 21, 2020. https://www.techtransparencyproject.org/articles/extremists-are-using-facebook-to-organize-for-civil-war-amid-coronavirus. Accessed August 4, 2020.

Wray, Christopher. "FBI Oversight." FBI, February 5, 2020. https://www.fbi.gov/news/testimony/fbioversight-020520 Accessed August 4, 2020.

Woolard, Brett. "Criminal Complaint Carrillo." June 15, 2020. https://www.justice.gov/opa/press-release/file/1285706/download. Accessed August 4, 2020.

# Index

active shooter training 65–6
al-Qaeda 9, 14
American Academy of Surgeons 62
American Civil Liberties Union (ACLU) 19
*American Psycho* (movie) 59
Anchondo, Andre 53
Anchondo, Jordan 53
anomia (disaffection with society) 84
Antifa movement 87
Ardern, Jacinda 99
Arendt, Hannah 89
assault weapons 61
attitude polarization 86

Barr, William 57
Biden, Joe 61
bin Landen, Osama 85
*Bipartisan Background Checks Act of 2019* 61
Black Lives Matter (BLM) movement 80, 97, 100
Boogaloo extremists 96–7
Brady, James 60
Brady, Sarah 60
*Brady Handgun Violence Protection Act* (a.k.a. *Brady Bill*) (1993) 60
*Breakin' 2: Electric Boogaloo* (movie) 96
Brookings Institute 16
Bureau of Alcohol, Tobacco, Firearms and Explosives (ATF) 57, 58

Central Intelligence Agency (CIA) 17
*The Chapman Survey of American Fears*
(CSAF) 4, 5, 11, 19, 53, 55, 63, 65, 81, 95
civil liberties violations 18–9, 95
Clinton, Hillary 86
*CNN* 80, 98
Collaborative for Academic, Social, and Emotional Learning (CASEL) 68
conspiracy theories 3, 4, 5–6, 78–90; COVID-19 80; crisis actor conspiracy 78–9; factors contributing to belief in 81–6; mass shooting as staged event 78–9; numbers who believe in 81; simplification of 99
COVID-19 pandemic 1, 56, 58, 80, 87, 88, 96, 97, 100
crippled epistemology 85

Delahanty, Thomas 60
Department of Homeland Security 3, 10, 15, 16, 18, 19, 57
Department of Justice 12, 57

Eastman, Alexander 62
Elass, H. Jaymi 89
Epstein, Jeffrey 87
Europol 4
extreme risk protection orders (ERPOs) (a.k.a. red flag laws) 61–2, 97

Facebook 9, 10, 78, 79, 80, 96, 97, 99
fake news 89
false flag attacks 3–4, 78, 84, 88
fear of being mass shooting victim 53, 54–5; increase in gun sales and 55–6

Federal Bureau of Investigation (FBI) 9, 10, 17, 55, 61, 89, 95, 96
First Amendment of US Constitution activities 19
4chan 6, 78
Fourth Amendment of US Constitution 69
*Fox News* 81, 87
freedom of speech and assembly 13–4
fusion centers 17, 18; criticisms of 18–9

*The Gateway Pundit* (blog) 78
Gen Z activism 100
*Gil v. DOJ* (Challenge to Government's Suspicious Activity Reporting Program, 2014) 19
GoFundMe 79
Gonzalez, Emma 67, 98
*Google* 78, 87
Gordon, Mark 65
Green, Tony 88
*The Guardian* 79
Gun Control Act (1968) 60
gun control measures 4, 53, 58, 59–60, 67; arming school employees 69; background checks 57–8, 60; government policies 53; school groups' 67–8
gun sales 54–5; COVID-19 pandemic and increase in 56–7, 58; as essential businesses 57; increase in from fear 55; mass media coverage of mass shootings and 55
gun violence 1, 97, 98; lives lost to 62
gun violence restraining order (GRVO, California) 61, 62

Hartford Consensus 62
Heyer, Heather 16
Hofstadter, Richard 86, 87
Hogg, David 80
HONR Network 6

*Infowars* 6, 78
Ingraham, Lauran 80
*Instagram* 97
ISIS 10
Islamaphobia 96
Islamic extremism 14, 17

*jihad* (struggle) 18
Jihadists 14, 17
Jones, Alex 6, 78, 80, 81

Kennedy, John F 81
*Know The Signs* (video) 68

Lankford, Adam 99
Lee, Robert E 15, 16

MacAdam, Wade 66
*March For Our Lives* student-led advocacy group 67
mass media 2–3; gun purchases and shootings coverage 55; role in mass shootings 99–100
mass shootings:; *see also* school shootings; Charleston, South Carolina 58, 95; Christchurch, New Zealand 54, 61, 95, 99; Dayton, Ohio 1, 54; El Paso, Texas 1, 53, 95; fear of 4–5, 95; Gilroy, California 54; increase of 1, 53; Las Vegas, Nevada 1, 4, 5, 78, 79, 81, 82; Orlando, Florida 1; Pittsburgh, Pennsylvania 1, 4, 59, 95; San Bernardino, California 1, 54; Sutherland Springs, Texas 3, 4; Thousand Oaks, California 1
Matejka, Braden 79
McCarthy, Timothy 60
*Memory Hole Blog* 80
monological belief systems 85–6

*The National Commission on Terrorist Attacks Upon the United States (a.k.a. The 9/11 Commission)* 17–8
National Instant Criminal Background Check System (NICS) 57, 58
*National Public Radio (NPR)* 80
National Rifle Association (NRA) 3, 57, 58, 59, 60, 61, 62, 67, 69, 70, 80, 98
Nationwide Suspicious Activity Reporting Initiative 18
*Natural Born Killers* (movie) 59
*Never Again MSD* student-led advocacy group 67
9/11 attacks on US 1, 9, 17; *The 9/11 Commission* 17–8
*1984* (Orwell) 89

# Index

*Nobody Dies at Sandy Hook: It was a FEMA Drill Designed to Promote Gun Control* (Fetzer) 80
No Notoriety campaign 98, 99
North Carolina Information Sharing & Analysis Center 18
Nugent, Ted 80

Obama, Barack 58, 88
Orwell, George 89

*The Paranoid Style in American Politics* (Hofstadter) 86
peer influence 86
Peinovich, Mike "Enoch" 16
Pelosi, Nancy 61
Phillip, Tanzil 100
Pickney, George C 58
Pomeroy, Frank 3
Pozner, Leonard 6, 80
Pozner, Noah 80
*Proofs of Conspiracy Against All the Religions and Governments of Europe Carried on in the Secret Meetings of Free Masons, Illuminati, and Reading Societies* (a.k.a. *Bavarian Illuminati*) 86
public education 2, 4, 20, 62, 95; reporting of suspicious activity 13

QAnon 87, 89

racially/ethnically motivated violent extremists (RMVEs) 96
Rapert, Jason 88
Razak, Tariq 19
*Ready Houston* training video 65
Reagan, Nancy 60
Reagan, Ronald 60
*Reddit* 6, 99
Reich, Sabrina 66
Re-Open rallies 97
retaliation, fear of 11–2
*The Right Stuff* podcast 16
right-wing extremists 100
*Run. Hide. Fight.* training video 64, 65

Sandy Hook Promise *Know the Signs* Programs 68
Schildkraut, Jaclyn 98
school lockdown drills 66

school shootings: active shooter training for 65–6; Columbine High School, Colorado 60, 98, 99; followers 89; guns in schools and 69–70; increase in 1; Marjory Stoneman Douglas High School, Parkland, Florida 67, 69, 80, 81, 82, 98, 99, 100; numbers of in US compared to other countries 5; as pop culture objects 98; Sandy Hook Elementary School, Newtown, Connecticut 5, 54, 58, 62, 68, 79, 80, 81, 82, 98; Sangus High School, Santa Clarita, California 63; signs to watch out for 68; Virginia Tech, Blacksburg, Virginia 98; as worry for youth 66
Schultz, Debbie Wasserman 57
Second Amendment of US Constitution 58, 67
See Something, Say Something campaign 2, 5, 10–1, 68, 95; increase in public awareness of 11; outreach efforts for 11; public perceptions and 12–3; retaliation fears and 11–2
self-image 85
South Dakota plane crash (1993) 81
Southern Poverty Law Center 96
Stop the Bleed initiative 2, 4–5, 62, 63, 64, 65
Sunstein, Cass 85
suspicious activity reports (SARS) 18, 19

terrorism 1; balancing civil liberties and safety to curb 20–1; domestic 15–6, 89, 95, 96; fear of 4–5; public information to help prevent 9–10; Trump administration response to domestic 16–7; in the US 14–5
Teves, Alex 98
totalitarianism 89
Trudeau, Justin 61
Trump, Donald 15, 16, 17, 57, 59, 69, 88, 89, 96
Trump, Eric 87
*Twitter* 80, 81

Unite the Right rallies 15

video games 59

*Violent Crime Control and Law Enforcement Act of 1994* 61

white supremacists 14, 17, 61, 95, 100; Charlottesville, Virginia 15–6

Wray, Christopher 95

*YouTube* 6, 78, 80, 88, 99